Advance Praise for *Solitary Séance*

"The era of direct contact with the spirit realm has opened, and Raymond Buckland has written the perfect book for it! Buckland brings his wonderful wisdom, insight, and experience together in this comprehensive guide for personal spirit communications that you can pursue on your own anywhere, including right at home. Everyone interested in the paranormal should have this book!"

—Rosemary Ellen Guiley, author of
The Encyclopedia of Ghosts and Spirits

"Once again, Ray Buckland has given the true seeker a valuable tool for development. *Solitary Séance* is a 'must have' for anyone wanting to incorporate spirit communication into his or her life. These exercises and explanations lead readers to where they need to go in order to create a solid connection with those in spirit. Bravo! This work truly opens the doors of spirit to let us know we are never alone."

—Dr. Patricia L. Bell, author of *Timeless Love: A Guide to Healing
Grief and Learning to Live Again*

"Drawing on his vast knowledge and expertise in this field, Raymond gives us a complete system of instruction for the solitary practitioner of mediumship while reviewing the history and tenets of Spiritualism, all with his usual wit and warmth. This book belongs in the hands of all serious inquirers. I highly recommend it."

—Most Rev. James F. Lagona, D.D., J.D.,
Orthodox Catholic bishop, medium, and healer

T0004928

Praise for *Buckland's Complete Book of Witchcraft*

"Based on Raymond Buckland's successful Seax-Wica Seminary course, this classic book is essential reading for all persons seriously interested in the art and religion of Witchcraft. The insight it provides is beneficial for solitaries and covens alike, making it well-deserving of a place in every Witch's personal library."

—Gerina Dunwich, author of
The Wicca Spellbook and *Wicca Craft*

"Never in the history of the Craft has a single book educated as many people, spurred as many spiritual paths, or conjured as much personal possibility as *Buckland's Complete Book of Witchcraft*. More than just a treasured classic, it is the one book that no seeker should ever be without!"

—Dorothy Morrison, author of *The Craft*

"This book was one of the first to guide me on the path of my Craft. Detailed yet non-threatening and educational yet fun . . . I highly recommend this book as an important introduction to the Craft in this modern age."

—Fiona Horne, author of *Witch: A Magickal Journey*
and TV/radio host

"A huge work of excellent materials. Buckland has lifted the last thin veil about Witchcraft, releasing it back into the mainstream to be a folk religion as it used to be."

—Z Budapest, activist and author of *Summoning the Fates*

"*Buckland's Complete Book of Witchcraft* is an excellent beginner book for someone interested in traditional Wicca, especially if they are interested in practicing their religion as part of a circle or coven."

—eCauldron.net

About the Author

Born in London, England, Raymond Buckland has written over sixty books—fiction and nonfiction—of which there are more than two million copies in print, with translations into seventeen languages. He has received many awards for his work, and his books have been featured by several national book clubs. Raymond has also written screenplays and has served as Technical Director for films, working with Orson Welles and William Friedkin (director of *The Exorcist*).

Raymond is a leading authority on the occult and the supernatural. He has lectured at colleges and universities across the country, and he has been the subject of articles in such newspapers and magazines as the *New York Times*, the *Los Angeles Times*, *Cosmopolitan*, *True*, and many others. He has also been a guest on numerous radio and television talk shows, including *The Dick Cavett Show*. He has appeared extensively on stage in Great Britain and has played small character parts in movies in the United States. His recent books include *Buckland's Book of Spirit Communications* and *Signs, Symbols & Omens*.

Raymond is listed in a number of reference works, including *Contemporary Authors*, *Who's Who in America*, and *Men of Achievement*. He lives on a small farm in north-central Ohio, with his wife, Tara, and two Chihuahua dogs.

Solitary Séance

How You Can
Talk with Spirits
on Your Own

RAYMOND BUCKLAND

Llewellyn Publications
Woodbury, Minnesota

First Edition
Tenth Printing, 2022

Cover illustration © Istvan Orosz/Marlena Agency; Border © iStockphoto
.com/Cloudniners
Cover design by Lisa Novak
Editing by Brett Fechheimer

The domino interpretations on pp. 144–150 first appeared in *The Fortune-Telling Book: The Encyclopedia of Divination and Soothsaying* by Raymond Buckland. Copyright © 2004 Visible Ink Press®, reprinted by permission.

Complete list of art credits can be found on page 229

Llewellyn is a registered trademark of Llewellyn Worldwide Ltd.

Library of Congress Cataloging-in-Publication Data
Buckland, Raymond.
Solitary séance : how you can talk with spirits on your own / Raymond Buckland. — 1st ed.
   p. cm.
Includes bibliographical references (p.   ).
ISBN 978-0-7387-2320-4
1. Spiritualism. 2. Seances. I. Title.
BF1261.2B785 2011
133.9—dc22
                        2010044211

Llewellyn Worldwide Ltd. does not participate in, endorse, or have any authority or responsibility concerning private business transactions between our authors and the public.
   All mail addressed to the author is forwarded but the publisher cannot, unless specifically instructed by the author, give out an address or phone number.
   Any Internet references contained in this work are current at publication time, but the publisher cannot guarantee that a specific location will continue to be maintained. Please refer to the publisher's website for links to authors' websites and other sources.

Llewellyn Publications
A Division of Llewellyn Worldwide Ltd.
2143 Wooddale Drive
Woodbury, MN 55125-2989
www.llewellyn.com

Printed in the United States of America

Other Books by Raymond Buckland

Advanced Candle Magick
Buckland's Book of Spirit Communications
Buckland's Complete Book of Witchcraft
Gypsy Dream Dictionary
Practical Candleburning Rituals
Scottish Witchcraft & Magick
Signs, Symbols & Omens
Witchcraft from the Inside

For Tara
and dedicated to my friends at
Lily Dale, New York

Contents

Introduction

In many people's minds, such words as *Spiritualism* and *séance* trigger visions of Ouija® boards, Victorian table-tipping, darkened rooms, and phony ghosts—the kinds of things relentlessly exploited in low-budget movies and shown on late-night television. Yet Spiritualism is a serious religion, philosophy, and science that has been practiced by intelligent people for well over one hundred and fifty years.

In this book I will look more closely at Spiritualism and the séance, and in particular examine ways in which the average person—*working alone*—can experiment with various aspects of spirit communication.

In recent times there have been many television specials and series about ghost-hunting, about finding ghosts

NSAC DEFINITION

Adopted by the National Spiritualist Association of Churches on October 24, 1951, the definitions of *Spiritualism* and of a *Spiritualist* are as follows:

"**Spiritualism** is a Science, Philosophy, and Religion of continuous life, based upon the demonstrated fact of communication, by means of mediumship, with those who live in the Spirit World. A **Spiritualist** is one who believes, as the basis of his or her religion, in the communication between this and the Spirit World by means of mediumship and who endeavors to mould his or her character and conduct in accordance with the highest teachings derived from such communication."

NSAC Spiritualist Manual, NSAC Lily Dale, 2002

in supposedly haunted houses. These programs, and carefully planned "documentaries," generally focus on getting rid of what are viewed as "unwanted guests." There seems to be little effort put into making contact and finding out why the spirit is there and then interacting with that spirit. There also seems to be little effort put into trying to contact a *specific* spirit—a deceased family member or close friend—and "conversing" with them.

It is erroneously believed that there must always be a medium present (a person trained in making that connection) in order to affect spirit contact. Yet in fact there are many ways to link with spirit that need not involve a medium—leastwise, not a professional medium. It is also generally believed that for personal contact there must be, at the very least, a minimum of two people: a medium and a sitter. Yet there are many forms of spirit communication that can be carried out very successfully by an individual, a person acting alone . . . that individual becoming both sitter *and* medium. *You* can be that person, and these are the forms of communication that we will be focusing on in this book.

I will start at the beginning in that I'll talk a little about death and dying and what it entails. Woody Allen said "I'm not afraid to die; I just don't want to be there when it happens!" That is the feeling of most people. They know that death is inevitable but really don't want to even think about it. Yet we all die; there's no escape! So what exactly does it mean to "die"?

In the Spiritualist belief, death is only a transition. It is a change from the physical world into which we were born and in which we matured, to the next "level," or world, where we continue in a spiritual form. We all have a spirit, soul, or spark within us. That spirit (and I will use the word *spirit* rather than *soul* throughout this book) is what lives on after this transition we term "death." It is that which, under certain circumstances, may be contacted by those still living here in the physical world.

In ancient Greece, the continued existence of the dead was dependent upon the continuing remembrance of the living. The Greek spirit world was a cold, grey, and dreary place known as *Hades* and ruled over by the god of that name. In ancient Rome, the afterworld was ruled over by Pluto. Both the ancient Greeks and the Romans made contact with their dead through the agencies of their priests. The ancient Egyptian priests, also, were intermediaries between humans and the gods, offering prayers and relaying messages. Many Buddhist and Confucian-influenced societies maintain a contact and even a veneration of the ancestors—not "praying" to them in the sense of worshipping them, for they are not viewed as deities, but "speaking" to them to show respect and honor.

Native Americans, Voudouns, Aboriginals, and many others maintain a connection with the world of departed spirits. The Mayans and the Aztecs had priests who were plenipotentiaries for the people, acting between the living and the dead. So there has certainly been contact with spirits of the dead for millennia. Yet there had been little, if any, evidence of *personal* communication, of one-on-one exchanges between the Physical World and the Spirit

SPIRIT AND SOUL

The eternal immaterial part of each and every person is an immeasurable unit known variously as the *spirit* or the *soul*. To some the two words are interchangeable, but to others there are subtle differences in the meanings. Spiritualists have no set belief on the subject. As in so much of Spiritualism, it is left to the interpretation of the individual. But I like the explanation given by Mary W. Matthews: "The human *mind* comprises the brain and all its workings—memory, perception, reason, the stew of hormones that results in our emotions. It is, in other words, the 'hardware' of human existence. The human *soul* is what governs the human hardware—the 'software' of human existence, our very own 'operating system' unique to each of us. The human *spirit* is the 'electricity' that animates us."*

* Mary W. Matthews, "The Difference Between Soul and Spirit"

World, until as recently as the mid-nineteenth century, and an incident in Hydesville, New York. This—because of this very personal communication—is regarded as the birth of Modern Spiritualism.

We are *all* potential mediums. We all have the ability to be that conduit between the two worlds. We may not all be as *practiced* as a professional medium, but then we don't need to be making the connection with spirit except on a few occasions, and then strictly for our own benefit or for the benefit of those close to us. It is somewhat akin to acknowledging that there are professional musicians whom we would happily pay to go and listen to in a concert hall, yet we are still able to return home and play the piano (or whatever other instrument) quite happily for our own entertainment. The professional may give a stirring interpretation of Beethoven's Piano Concerto #5 in E Flat Major while we struggle through "Chopsticks," but the professional can be the tremendous inspiration leading to our satisfaction and feeling of accomplishment with our own performance.

A glance at the contents of this book might suggest that this is simply a work on divination or fortunetelling. In many ways it is . . . but then, what is divination? The word is connected to *divinity*: the belief that it is a gift of the gods that provides the ability to peer into the future. Here, however, we take it a step further in ascribing the results to spirit. Spirit—perhaps acting through divinity—is providing the answers to questions posed.

Professional mediums seldom use physical tools for their mediumship, yet tools can be of benefit to help the less-practiced person obtain the same results. A professional medium sees clairvoyantly (for example) without any physical aids. Yet if that same medium were to gaze into a crystal ball in order to focus her attention and then produce the same results as when not using one, would there be anything wrong with that? No. *The sole reason for indulging in mediumship is to connect with spirit and to produce material of an evidential nature that will prove continued existence*—the certitude of a life after the transition we term "death." It should not matter, then, exactly *how* that material is produced. If using some physical object as a focal point can help produce that evidential material, then why not use it? And when you are acting alone, without any sort of an audience, it may well be especially beneficial to work with specific tools in order to be assured of getting the best results you can.

With the exercises in this book, we are not using these tools for simple divination or fortunetelling but are using them to bridge that gap between the physical world and the world of spirit. Here, "divination tools" will become "medium's tools."

"But wait! What about danger? Are there dangers associated with this spirit communication?" These are common fears and, not to take them lightly, I would say that they are generally unfounded. Having said that, I would add that it doesn't hurt to take reasonable precautions. To that end I will start by telling you how to create what is known as an "Egg of Protection": a psychic shield that will keep at bay any and all negative energies that might find their way into your personal space.

There is no special work place needed for what is taught in this book. You don't have to establish a "temple" or even a "séance room"; you don't need to have an altar with a variety of altar tools. As will be explained, you can achieve outstanding results with absolutely no tools at all. But where it might help to have some assistance, then I will tell you how best to go about it.

The most important thing is to remain open-minded and, especially, to be open to spirit. So many deceased loved ones and acquaintances have passed on that there are bound to be those who would like nothing better than to have a conversation with you again. To relive the past, perhaps to pass on a message or messages to others, to explain what might be puzzling those left behind . . . there are so many reasons for spirits to want to contact us, never mind the reasons we may have for wanting to contact them. So stay open to them; whether or not you have received any evidence, stay open to the possibility of it coming.

How do you allow spirit to come? That is the main substance of this book. There are a large number of ways to allow spirit to make contact. Some you will find work extremely well for you, while others will seem to give no results. The only thing to do is to experiment, to try the many different methods suggested and see what works and what does not. Don't just try something once and then, when nothing happens, reject it. Give it a chance. Try different methods at different times, under different circumstances. I would advise working with just one method at a time, but you could certainly experiment with, say, three or four over the course of a week, one a day, and then repeat them over a number of weeks. This way you can find not only what works but what you feel most comfortable with. Once you have established your most effective method(s), then work consistently with that, keeping careful records of all you obtain.

I do urge you to keep records. Keep notes of any and all attempts you make to communicate with spirit, whether or not those attempts seem to be successful. Quite often it will seem that you have received nothing of any substance, yet when you review what came through—perhaps days or even weeks later—you may be surprised at the number of small points of interest that can add up to major revelations.

Alone or with others? Much of the attraction of contacting the departed lies in sharing with others what it is that you receive. These exercises certainly may be done by groups—by more than one person. But the whole point of this book is to present methods for the *individual* to communicate, with no outside help. There have been no books such as this offered anywhere before. The vast majority deal with working with others, either as a sitter or as a developing medium. This book will most certainly help you develop as a medium, if that is your wish, but its principal goal is to allow you to make that spirit contact without having to rely on anyone else. As I mention in the next chapter, I have seen people who go to a Spiritualist camp in order to have a sitting with a medium and then become most upset when the summer season of that camp comes to an end and they are no longer able to have such sittings. It was such a situation that inspired me to write this book, so that people need not wait for the next season, or the next available medium, but can continue contact with the Spirit World by themselves.

In my 2004 book *Buckland's Book of Spirit Communications*, I present an intensive course on mediumship development and Spiritualism, for both individuals and groups. This present volume, by contrast, focuses on what can be done by the *individual*, working alone, on a regular or just an occasional basis. There are obvious parallels and a few repetitions, but it will be seen that the two books do complement each other.

—Raymond Buckland

Preliminaries

At such Spiritualist communities as Lily Dale, New York; Camp Chesterfield, Indiana; Harmony Grove, California, and many others, the streets are filled, during camp season, with people walking from one medium to another. At the end of the season there is an almost discernible rush to get a reading before it's too late. Too late, that is, in the sense that most of the mediums close up for the winter. So, what to do when there is no medium available? The answer is . . . become your own medium.

This is not as unlikely as it may at first seem. We all have the potential to be mediums; we all have the ability to make contact with spirit. Some find it easier than others, but all—with a little practice—have the ability. Let's examine the possibilities.

What is "death"?

Many people go out of their way not to say the words *death*, *dead*, or *dying*. They speak of a loved one "passing over," being "lost," or "making the transition." What they *mean* is that the person is dead . . . that's it! It's just a matter of semantics. It all means the same, so why not use the basic, very simple, word? It doesn't make the "loss" of the loved one any easier to accept. It doesn't ease the passing. I'm sure most will continue to use these euphemisms, but here, in this book, I will call a spade a spade and speak of death and dying.

So what takes place at death? It is the departure of the spirit from the body-shell it has inhabited throughout its time on this physical plane. When the spirit has departed, the body is simply an empty shell and what becomes of it is mainly a matter of tradition. In many societies, the tradition is either to bury it or burn it. Some Native American tribes in the Great Plains region would lay out the body on a raised platform, allowing the vultures and carrion-eaters to feast on it. Others, such as the Northeast Iroquois, saved the skeletons for a mass burial with clothing and ornaments for use in the afterlife. There were many variations, not just among the Native Americans but with different peoples around the world. But regardless of what is done with the body, the spirit moves on.

Moves on to where? To the next plane of existence. Andrew Jackson Davis coined the term *Summerland* for this afterlife world. I will just stick with *Spirit World*. From all the accounts that we have, through mediums, the Spirit World is very much like this physical one, although its make-up, and the very act of existence there, can be greatly changed by the individual. It seems that initially, at least, we find exactly what we expect to find. Then, gradually, spirits are brought to see that not everything is exactly as they were taught. In this way there is no great shock to them passing over. If you had a lifetime of being assured—by your religion, for example—that there is no such thing as reincarnation, then it could be a tremendous shock to die and find out that in fact there *is* reincarnation . . . or vice versa: believing that there is reincarnation and then finding that there is not. (In Spiritualism there is no specific teaching on this subject, the individual being left to make up his or her own mind.) So, reincarnation—and other major beliefs—may or may not be a fact, but it will take a while in the afterlife to find out.

The descriptions of the Spirit World have been fairly consistent from mediums. In his *General Course of the*

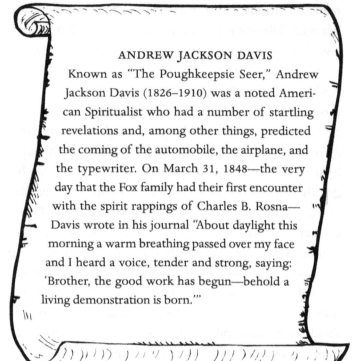

ANDREW JACKSON DAVIS

Known as "The Poughkeepsie Seer," Andrew Jackson Davis (1826–1910) was a noted American Spiritualist who had a number of startling revelations and, among other things, predicted the coming of the automobile, the airplane, and the typewriter. On March 31, 1848—the very day that the Fox family had their first encounter with the spirit rappings of Charles B. Rosna—Davis wrote in his journal "About daylight this morning a warm breathing passed over my face and I heard a voice, tender and strong, saying: 'Brother, the good work has begun—behold a living demonstration is born.'"

History, Science, Philosophy and Religion of Spiritualism, Thomas Grimshaw writes, "The Spirit World is a real world, just as real to spirits functioning through their spirit bodies as the physical world is to us who function through our physical bodies."[1] Journalist and Spiritualist Maurice Barbanell said, "There are no hard and fast boundaries between this world and what is wrongly called the next. They are both parts of one universe, and these aspects mingle and blend and merge all the time."[2]

Where and when did spirit contact start?

From the earliest days of prehistory, when humans were living in caves, there was a belief in a life after death. Early humans, such as the Gravettians, buried their dead with clothing, tools, and weapons so that they would have them available in the afterlife. Much later, the ancient Egyptians, for example, made elaborate tombs with all the accouterments of everyday living on hand, ready for the dead. The community graves of Neolithic times placed personal possessions alongside the bodies. Anglo-Saxon graves of the sixth and seventh centuries, like the one unearthed at Sutton Hoo, in Woodbridge, Suffolk, England, contained a wealth of objects buried with the deceased, presumably for use in the afterlife, the Spirit World. Priests of various cultures claimed to be able to speak with the gods and even to make contact with the

---

1. Grimshaw, *General Course of the History, Science, Philosophy and Religion of Spiritualism*, 5.
2. Barbanell, *This Is Spiritualism*, 24.

FOX FAMILY

An outbreak of bangs and rappings on the walls of a small house in upstate New York on Friday, March 31, 1848, was what projected two young girls, Cathie (Kate) and Margaretta, and their mother, Margaret, into the limelight. They were the Fox family. It wasn't that such rappings were new—many of their neighbors admitted to having had similar experiences—but it was that when ten-year-old Kate started asking questions, the "rapper" *gave intelligent answers!* A conversation developed.

Neighbors who were called in to witness what was happening likewise received answers to questions they asked, and even when the two girls and their mother left the house (to stay at a neighbor's for the night), the ever-growing crowd of people continued to have intelligent communication with the rapper. This entity turned out to be the spirit of a murdered peddler, Charles B. Rosna, whose body was later discovered bricked-up in the basement.

In the following weeks and months, methods of communicating were fine-tuned, and, in many demonstrations, the girls went on to show their ability to make contact with a variety of spirits. Soon others, emboldened by the Fox sisters, admitted to similar abilities and also gave demonstrations.

Sir Arthur Conan Doyle, in his book *The History of Spiritualism*, said: "It was no new gift [the Fox sisters] exhibited, it was only that their courageous action in making it widely known made others come forward and confess that they possessed the same power. This universal gift of mediumistic faculties now for the first time began to be freely developed."

dead. Yet it was not until the mid-nineteenth century—in Western civilization at least—that regular two-way communication between the living and the deceased was established.

In the early 1800s, as in previous centuries, many people heard "ghostly noises": banging and thumping, scratching and scraping. In Hydesville, New York, on March 31, 1848, a "conversation" developed, which is hailed as the birth of Modern Spiritualism. Later, others took the same approach and found that they too were able to exchange information with contacting spirits. Spirit communication became a movement and then a religion—one that is thriving today.

Religion or practice?

Spiritualism is a belief in the continuation of life after the transition known as death. It is a belief not only that death is not the end but also that it is possible to make contact with the departed spirits. Such contact is a practice in and of itself and may be exercised by anyone.

Yet in the early days following the Fox family's breakthrough, many enthusiasts made the movement into a religion, inspiring a variety of Spiritualist churches. This religious movement became very big in the United States and Great Britain, as well as in other parts of the world.

The religion of Spiritualism is a monotheistic belief system, though it acknowledges the divine feminine along with the masculine. Spiritualism is practiced through various denominational Spiritualist churches, primarily in the United States and Great Britain. Most hold that it is a religion in its own right, but some few churches (mainly in the U.K.) do align themselves with Christianity, terming themselves "Christian Spiritualists."

There are established (non-Christian) liturgies and a national organization in the U.S.—the National Spiritualist Association of Churches (NSAC)—with training programs for mediums, healers, ministers, teachers, and others. Although following practices similar to the Christian ones of Sunday services, with the singing of hymns and a sermon or talk by a distinguished person, the Spiritualist services do differ from those of Christianity. Always included as part of the service is a demonstration of contact with spirit given by a registered medium.

There is a strong belief in personal responsibility for one's actions, with no recognition of a soul's assignment to a Heaven or Hell. It is thought that no soul is irredeemable, believing that the spark of divinity dwells within all, and that all should try to mold their character and conduct "in accordance with the highest teachings derived from such communication" with the Spirit World, in the words of one of the NSAC's definitions. The practices of mediumship and of healing are integral to the religion.

The time seemed to be ripe for this new religion. In upstate New York, in 1855, the old religious organization known as the Free Thinkers reorganized as the Laona Free Association. By 1871 the group was having regular camp meetings alongside Lake Cassadaga, on land owned by one Willard Alden. A few years later the group bought its own land nearby, and along with the temporary tents constructed a permanent stable and some cottages. From midsummer weekend gatherings, by 1877 the season had been extended until late September. Despite terrible rain that year, the crowds were bigger than ever.

The name of the meeting area became known as the Cassadaga Free Assembly, and then the City of Lights, and, more recently, Lily Dale Assembly (for the large number of water lilies on the lake). As time went on, there came the need for a hotel of some sort, so the stable was commandeered and (in what was then known as "hung suspension") lifted up so that a second floor could be built underneath it. This method was to be repeated in later years for a third floor, the present Hotel Maplewood, at Lily Dale, having that original stable as its top floor.

Other Spiritualist communities came into being and developed in other parts of New York, and in Ohio, Indi-

LILY DALE

Originally named the Laona Free Association when it was formed on December 3, 1855, the association was a reorganization of the older Religious Society of Free Thinkers. Today it is the Lily Dale Assembly, a Spiritualist community situated on the banks of Lake Cassadaga, located in Chautauqua County in upstate New York. A village of some three hundred homes, it is the world's largest center for Spiritualist development and the practice of the Spiritualist religion. There are two hotels, a post office, fire department, restaurants, gift shops, and numerous guest houses. Two Spiritualist churches serve the community, with two or three more close by, outside the grounds. Throughout the summer months there is an intense program of workshops and lectures offered, together with free readings, healings, discussions, and the like. The churches continue the programs on a smaller scale throughout the rest of the year.

ana, and across the United States. Very quickly the news crossed the Atlantic, and Spiritualism started and grew in Great Britain and elsewhere. A finding of the 2001 UK Census showed that Spiritualism has emerged as Great Britain's eighth-largest religious group.

A variation known as *Spiritism* grew in France and from there extended to South America (Brazil especially) and the Philippines. Many thousands of people follow the religion of Spiritualism, in one form or another, and many more simply practice the various forms of communication without the religious aspects. Spiritualism is, then, both a practice and a religion.

One of the main appeals of Spiritualism is that it encourages self-exploration and learning. Bearing in mind that it is "descended" from the Free Thinkers of the nineteenth century, it is very much a "thinking person's" religion. As authors Rita S. Berkowitz and Deborah S. Romaine put it: "Spirit communication puts the quest for information into *your* hands. You determine what to ask, and what to do with the answers you receive."[3]

---

3. Berkowitz and Romaine, *The Complete Idiot's Guide to Communicating with Spirits*, 37.

Is there any danger in contacting spirits?

There is more danger in electrically wiring a house than there is in contacting spirits. Late-night television and low-budget movies have promoted the idea of danger from contacting the dead, or any other aspect of practicing "the occult"! (*Occult*, incidentally, simply means "secret" or "hidden.") It should be remembered that it is fear of the unknown that is exploited to promote these shows on the small and the large screen. If Spiritualist séances and the like were shown as they truly are—with no horror elements—then there would be nothing to attract a mass audience. The cognoscenti would find them fascinating, it is true, but not in enough numbers for box-office success.

One of the spiritual laws, or natural laws, is the Law of Attraction. This states that like attracts like. Applied to a séance it means that if you are the typical loving, good-living follower of the Golden Rule, then you will only attract similar beings to yourself. It is only the negative (I don't believe that anyone is truly "evil," and so I avoid use of that word), damaging, and destructive person who will attract harmful spirits.

What about the possibility of possession? In a séance situation in which a medium goes into a deep trance, there would appear to be the chance of possession. Yet in fact a medium's trance is an elective state; it is a state where the medium *allows* a spirit to enter and make use of (for example) vocal cords or muscle groups. At any time the medium can reject the spirit and reclaim full use of his or her body. True "possession" is when a negative spirit *invades* the body and takes over all functions against the wishes of the owner. This could happen to anyone at any time, not simply in a séance-room situation. Yet, in fact, true possession is extremely rare. The official exorcist for the city of Rome claims that he receives many long-distance telephone calls from people believing themselves to be possessed, but that he actually performs exorcisms "as rarely as possible."

One of the most useful tools for spirit communication is the talking board, or Ouija® board. This is often held up as an example of how "evil" spirits can attack you! But it makes me think of the scenes from low-budget movies in which someone with a scary voice telephones a woman home alone, and makes a variety of threats. The woman becomes more and more hysterical when all she has to do is to hang up the phone!

It's the same with any psychic/spiritual connection. If you don't like what you're getting . . . break the connection! If a spirit is so desperate to talk to someone that it monopolizes the connection—be it talking board or whatever—then end the sitting. If this spirit keeps turning up only to find itself cut off every time, then it will quickly realize it's not getting anywhere and will go elsewhere. I'll have more to say on that in the chapter about talking boards.

Getting Started

I have said that there is no real danger with spirit communication, but, having said that, I would urge you to always take some simple precautions in *any* practice concerning the Spirit World. If you visit a construction site, you don't expect anything large and heavy to fall on your head, but it still behooves you to wear a hard hat "just in case." Similarly, if you are going to a psychic fair, or having your tarot cards read, or sitting in a psychic development circle, or participating in a séance, then do the following simple precautionary meditation first. In fact, I do this exercise every single morning as part of my daily regimen. It then serves to protect me not only from any chance metaphysical connection but also from various encounters, such as with so-called "psychic vampires" (people who, consciously or unconsciously, can drain your energies from you just by being with you).

Constructing the "Egg" of Protection

Sit quietly with your feet flat on the floor, your legs uncrossed and your back straight. (I prefer to do this with my shoes removed.) Your hands may rest in your lap. Close your eyes and relax. Breathe in deeply, fully expanding your lungs. As you breathe in, imagine the positive earth energy that creates all things coming up out of the earth, through the foundations of the building where you sit and up through the floor to enter your body through your feet.

We all have a close affinity with the earth. All plants, trees, vegetation, and minerals are directly connected to the earth; all animal life is indirectly connected. In effect, we all come from the earth. I believe very much in the earth energy. I can feel it flowing through my body; I can feel it flowing through plants and trees. It is a very positive energy. Sitting as you are, you are directly connected to the earth. Its energy flows upward, through the soles of your feet, up your legs and into your body. Even if you are sitting in a tall building many floors above the ground, that same energy flows up through the structure of the building, through the floor, and into you. As you sit quietly I want you to breathe in deeply, feeling that energy coming into your body. You can see it, in your mind's eye, as a white light, a gold light, a blue light . . . whatever works for you. I will describe it as a white light.

As you breathe in, see/feel that light coming into you—traveling up your legs into your body, down your arms, and into your hands and up into your head. Feel it filling your entire body. And as you breathe out, feel all negativity leaving your body. You may see/sense this as a brown or grey light leaving you. Spend some time breathing in the good, positive energy of the white light and breathing out the negative energy of the brown light. Feel all the little aches and pains disappear as your body fills with the energy of the earth.

When you have completely filled your body with the white light, keep on breathing it in for a while and see that light extend *beyond* your body until you are sitting in an "egg" of the light. Eggs have a hard shell that protects the contents; this is what you have created, in a psychic sense. You are now sitting inside a psychic Egg of Protection. Any negativity directed at you from anyone or anywhere will be deflected away from you, protecting you, without you even being aware of it.

As I've mentioned, I do this every morning so that I'm all set up for the whole day. If you don't want to do it that regularly—although I do encourage it—then at the very least do this exercise before attending *any* psychic event.

Spirit guides

We all have a spirit guide, known to some as a *guardian angel*, *gatekeeper*, *doorkeeper*, or other similar terms. Many of us have more than one. For example, if you are involved in healing of any sort, then you probably have a second spirit guide who specializes in that (many times it is someone who was a doctor when on the physical plane). Depending on your interests, you may have need of specific guides of various sorts. But we all have at least one major guide who has been with us since our birth.

You may or may not be aware of this guide (some people claim they don't have one, but I think it far more likely that they simply have not had reason to experience contact with the guide). Through meditation and/or in dreams, you may become aware of your guide(s). Your guide is that "still, small voice of conscience" that you may become aware of at certain times. This is your guardian in that he or she watches over you and tries to protect you from negativity. In a séance situation, it is the guide who "keeps order" in the Spirit World, ensuring that you are not suddenly inundated with spirits wishing to communicate. You might imagine your spirit guide saying to the visiting spirits, "Take a number!"

Occasionally, a deceased family member or even a onetime close friend is your guide. Many people have Native American guides, presumably because of their lives so close to the earth, lives with an unspoiled knowledge of the forces of nature. As Rita Berkowitz says, "Spirit guides are always with us, whether or not we realize it, and . . . they are there to *guide*, not to control."[4]

In Spiritualist séance rooms it's not uncommon for the medium to first make contact with the spirit guide, who, in turn, will introduce the spirits who come through. But working by yourself, don't be surprised if your guide does not put in an appearance; don't be surprised if there is no obvious intervention and if the individual spirits come through by themselves. That's not to say that your guide won't be there, overseeing what is happening, but he or she may decide not to intrude on such an intimate connection.

Prayer

Spiritualism is not a Christian religion; it is a religion in its own right. One of the principles of Spiritualism is that we

---

4. Berkowitz and Romaine, 80.

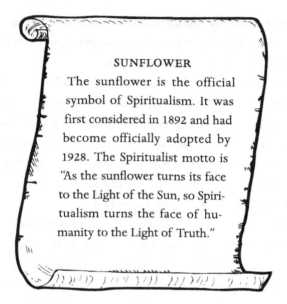

SUNFLOWER

The sunflower is the official symbol of Spiritualism. It was first considered in 1892 and had become officially adopted by 1928. The Spiritualist motto is "As the sunflower turns its face to the Light of the Sun, so Spiritualism turns the face of humanity to the Light of Truth."

are all accountable for our own actions. No one has been "saved" through the supposed actions or sacrifices of another.

Prayer is an expression of your thoughts and/or emotions and is not dictated by any supposed "authority." In some religions the act of prayer is ritualized and must follow a strict sequence of words and actions. There are even religions in which there is restriction on *who* may pray. Not so in Spiritualism. There is, in fact, encouragement to pray in your own words, as spontaneously as possible.

Words that come from the heart are far more powerful than those written down by someone else and printed in a book to be read at specific times. In your solitary séance, therefore, pray as you *feel* and for your own satisfaction. Don't worry about correct grammar, sentence construction, or the like; say what comes into your head.

However, one important question might be: to *whom* are you praying? Is it the Christian concept of an all-male deity or the Pagan/Neopagan belief in a Mother Goddess? Or are you following ideas of shamanism or animal totemism? It doesn't matter what it is; there is no "correct answer," as long as you are comfortable in what you do. In Spiritualism most prayers begin with "Father/Mother God," embracing the divine feminine as well as the masculine.

Meditation

Meditation is an important tool, whether for spirit communication or just for mental and physical well-being. Meditation differs from prayer, in that prayer is frequently an asking (of deity) for what you feel you need or for what you want to happen. Meditation complements prayer in that it is a "listening," possibly for the answer to that prayer. You don't have to spend a long time meditating, though some people do, but I would recommend a minimum of ten minutes a day. Try always to meditate at the same time of day, be it morning, afternoon, or evening.

I advocate starting every day with a meditation. You can go into it quite effortlessly from doing the white light "egg" building. Once your breathing has returned to normal, and you feel happy with the Egg of Protection that you have built, then try to make your mind blank. This is not easy—thoughts of all sorts will keep creeping in. Gently push them out again and focus on your breathing. Any thoughts that are truly important—any urgent messages from spirit—*will* make their way through to you, in one form or another. But don't *try* to receive anything at this stage. Just relax your whole body and try to think of nothing.

Some people will repeat a *mantra* in their head, over and over. A mantra can be simply a sound, not an actual word but more like a made-up word that has a pleasant feel to it—something that has no specific meaning to you. Continue this relaxation for about ten minutes. You don't need to spend too long at this. It's really to settle your mind, but the positive effects will last all day. It's too easy to get caught up in the idea of making contact with spirit yet being so disorganized that you can't focus on one particular loved one. Meditation seems to put everything into perspective. When you feel comfortable, then you may want to offer a short prayer (optional) and bring the meditation session to a close.

Format

The format of your séance is entirely up to you. I will suggest a procedure, but please feel free to experiment and to decide what works best for you. Make sure that you are in a situation that is "safe," in that you are not likely to be interrupted. Turn off your cell phone, television, radio, and anything else that is likely to interrupt you.

The time of day for your séance is important. Evening is usually best but not essential; it is best in that the "vibrations" seem more conducive for spirit communication. You may have noticed that in the evening—especially the late evening—you can pick up radio waves from far greater distances than you can during the daytime.

Consistency is another ingredient for success. If you have your séance every Wednesday (let's say) at 9:00 p.m., then spirit will get used to the fact that this is the best time to make contact.

I like to have a mild incense burning. I find that the scent helps create an atmosphere conducive to communing with spirit. Some people are allergic to incense, and in that case I suggest having aromatic flowers in the room. You might want to have flowers present anyway; I think it's

THE CLAIRS

There are various types of mediumship. Among them are what are known as "The Three Clairs": clairvoyance, clairaudience, and clairsentience. *Clair* is French for "clear." We have, then, clairvoyance, or clear-seeing; clairaudience, or clear-hearing; and clairsentience, or clear-sensing. A clairvoyant medium will *see* the spirits who make contact and can describe them in detail, but may not be able to hear anything they say. A clairaudient medium, however, can hear what the spirits have to say, but is unable to see them. A clairsentient "senses" the spirits and what message they are trying to impart. Sometimes a medium can be both clairvoyant *and* clairaudient, for example, but not always.

a nice addition. I also suggest low light for your sitting. I use candles. It doesn't have to be totally dark, but lowered light again seems to help create the best atmosphere. Some people eschew candles and use a low-wattage red light.

Depending upon which method I am practicing, I usually sit at what might be regarded as an altar, though to my mind that's not what it is in this setting. Since it's not the central focal point for a religious ceremony, I certainly wouldn't label it as such. If nothing else, it is a convenient table for holding any necessary paraphernalia (incense, candles, mirror . . . again, depending upon what I am practicing). It can be low—almost or totally on the floor—or it can be as high as a kitchen or dining table, or you might not need anything at all.

Start with your meditation, building the white light, and then proceed to a gentle singing. The songs should be upbeat—in other words, not the dirges sometimes found in church music but something melodic, light, and even humorous. You may prefer to simply hum. If you play an instrument—guitar, recorder, or whatever—there's no reason why you shouldn't utilize that.

The point here is to calm yourself and settle yourself into a comfortable space into which spirit will be drawn. Sound, color, light, aroma, and mental focus all play a part.

Decide before you start who it is that you would like to contact. If you have a photograph of the person, a drawing or painting, a letter in their handwriting, or any personal item that belonged to the person, then have that lying on the table. As you finish singing, address the spirit

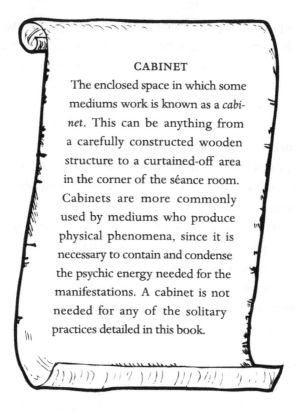

CABINET

The enclosed space in which some mediums work is known as a *cabinet*. This can be anything from a carefully constructed wooden structure to a curtained-off area in the corner of the séance room. Cabinets are more commonly used by mediums who produce physical phenomena, since it is necessary to contain and condense the psychic energy needed for the manifestations. A cabinet is not needed for any of the solitary practices detailed in this book.

by name and invite him or her to join you. I'd suggest that you speak out loud, but if you prefer you can do the calling mentally. I do find, however, that by vocalizing you are more able to focus on your desires.

Initially, call upon only one spirit at a time. When you've been conducting your séances for a while and feel completely comfortable with the process, then you can expand and invite a second spirit after the first has left. I'd suggest not trying to converse with more than one spirit at the same time; it could become bewildering. Even in everyday life, it can get confusing when more than one person tries to speak at the same time.

Record-keeping

One thing that is very important is record-keeping. You should keep a note of everything you do, every spirit contact that you make—including the ones that don't work out—and what information comes through. If you don't want to be writing while the séance is in progress, then have a tape recorder running, but I'd recommend transcribing what is on the tape as soon as possible afterward.

Many times there is information that comes through that is not immediately identifiable. Facts may have to be checked, names verified. This can be done later . . . the next day or whenever is most convenient. Much of the fun and excitement of spirit contact is in researching the information that spirit provides and then celebrating the successes.

Walk before you run

In what follows in this book I give a number of different methods that can be used by an individual to make contact with spirit. Some of them are more involved than others. Some are little more than ways to obtain brief messages while others are for continuous contact and communication. I encourage you to try them all . . . but not all at once!

Take any one method—let's say working with the pendulum, for example. Work with the pendulum for a number of sessions; I'd suggest at least eight or ten. If you have your séances once a week, then that would be over a ten-week period. If you get good results, then you might want to simply stick with that; you certainly don't *have* to try more than one method. But if you move on to another method—let's say working with automatic writing—then keep trying that one for a number of weeks. In this way you can try a variety of methods and can ensure that whatever you try has been given every opportunity to work.

Dreams

The most common method of connecting with spirit is through your dreams. Dreams are more than "night-time movies" to entertain you. Suppose that a good friend dies in an automobile accident . . . you may very well find that you dream of him or her for many nights—perhaps even several weeks—afterward. But these are not simple "dreams," as I've said; they are actual contacts from your friend's spirit, letting you know that he or she is there with you still.

Start a dream journal. This will be a detailed record of all your dreams. Keep a notebook, or pad of paper, beside your bed, together with a pen or pencil. *As soon as you wake up in the morning*, write down what you remember of your dreams. Do this immediately. Don't wait until you've rolled out of bed and staggered into the kitchen for that first cup of coffee! The longer you wait, the more your unconscious mind will tweak the dream remembrance. It will add bits to it and erase areas that it feels you may not be able to handle. So write down everything you can recall as soon as you wake up.

Of course, you may remember nothing! That does happen. In that case, just make a notation that you don't remember anything. It doesn't mean you didn't dream; it's just that you have no recollection of the dreams.

Over a relatively short period of time, you will find that you remember what you dream in greater and greater detail, and you will probably be surprised to find that you have many visits from departed spirits, meaningful to you, in those dreams. Sometimes you'll just have a confused jumble of a number of dreams, all mixed together and making no sense at all. Be patient and persevere. Pay special attention to the spirit visitations . . . in the dream, is spirit giving you information? Is he or she asking questions?

If there is one departed spirit in particular that you'd like to contact, then get into the habit of focusing your attention on that person as you fall asleep. It may help to have a photograph of the person beside your bed, where you can study it before turning out the light. Don't be afraid to address such a picture out loud. Let the person know that he or she is missed and loved. If you have questions, then ask them. You may have to do this for a number of nights in a row, but you'll find that the spirit will come through in your dreams and respond to your question(s).

Dream symbology can play an important part. When spirit finds that you are not aware of its presence, then it frequently brings into play symbols that *will* be noticed and that will help provide the message that it is trying to bring through.

There are many books of dream symbols available; some are good, but most are not very useful. The thing to keep in mind is that you cannot simply look up a dream symbol and say, "Ah, so that's what it means." Symbols in dreams—especially when directed by spirit—are very personal. You must therefore examine any symbol and determine whether it is a personal symbol or a universal symbol. I elaborated on this in my book *Gypsy Dream Dictionary*:[5]

> *There are two kinds of symbols that come through to us in our dreams:* universal *symbols and* personal *symbols.*
>
> *Suppose you dream about a castle. Now it could well be that you watch a lot of late-night television and see many old movies featuring vampires, ghosts, Satanists, or ogres of one sort or another living in castles. From this it could be that you automatically associate castles with evil. . . . Yet you could have a close friend who is interested in architecture and considers the castle to be a thing of beauty; the height of the architect's craft. For him or her the association of castles with evil is ridiculous. A third*

---

5. pp. 15–18.

person might have grown up in Europe and actually have lived in a castle for a time. He or she considers them neither evil nor beautiful but simply cold, damp, and drafty!

So here there are three totally different reactions to castles. Obviously there could be more. These, then, are personal interpretations. . . .

Yet there is also a universal *symbolism for castles. They are associated with ambition. Ambition is one of the interpretations that would be used by the majority of people when they have no particularly strong, personal feelings about castles. . . .*

As Carl Jung said: "No dream symbol can be separated from the individual who dreams it."

There are, then, a number of things to consider when you examine any dream you have, especially one in which a deceased loved one has appeared. This is another reason why it's a good idea to write down what you remember. You can then go back and study the dream without—consciously or unconsciously—adding to it or changing it in any way.

Do check for any possible personal symbolism first. The symbol and/or its meaning may reflect on the name of the spirit (dreaming of fields, for example, may be spirit's way of emphasizing that the spirit is there, if his name was *Fields*); or it may tie in to some experience or place from the past or something that the spirit has in common with you.

Universal symbolism includes those things that remain true for all humankind throughout the ages. Included are colors, numbers, form, and sexual identity (i.e., male and female). They come from the super-consciousness and therefore are timeless. Transportation, for example, is the universal symbol of spiritual advancement. As material technology has advanced, the application of symbology has kept pace. So, transportation may take one of the modern forms of conveyance, such as rockets, planes, steamships, trains, or automobiles, or one of the timeless modes, such as riding on the back of an animal or simply walking.

Following are a number of the universal symbols encountered in dreams. If you are unable to find a connection, then look up the symbol here and see if you can see a connection with spirit or with yourself. For example, dreaming of an acorn, or acorns, might indicate that the spirit coming through to you experienced a long wait to have things work out the way she originally hoped, but that later (perhaps after her death) the results of her efforts far exceeded the original hopes.

A

Accordion: A happy time, possibly with dancing. Enjoyment in a job or pastime.

Ace: From a deck of cards, an ace of spades represents a scandal; ace of clubs, a lawsuit; ace of diamonds, a legacy; ace of hearts, a love affair.

Acorn: Plans will take (may have taken) a longer time than hoped to come to fruition, but when fulfilled will far exceed what was hoped for.

Adoration: To be the object of adoration in a dream means that you (or spirit) used to flirt a lot.

Airplane: Spiritual advancement. This would indicate that spirit has advanced since his or her death. Perhaps in life he or she was not greatly interested in spiritual matters but now can see and appreciate their value.

Alarm clock: Spirit was never able to complete all the things that he or she wanted to do. It may also be spirit warning you that now is the time for action.

Altar: A focal point. Peace. Prosperity.

Ambulance: In spirit's past there may have been an accident, of one sort or another, that was significant.

Anchor: An anchor can be seen as something that held back spirit, or something that gave security; a foundation.

Apple: There are many associations with apples—"an apple for the teacher," "the apple associated with Adam and Eve," "the apple balanced on the head of William Tell's son," and so on. See how any of these might apply to spirit.

Apron: Indicates domesticity, or taking orders from another but getting satisfaction from it.

Armor: A suit of armor symbolizes security or worry about lack of security.

Arrow: Swift, silent, and can be deadly.

Ass/donkey: A quarrel between friends. If trotting, disappointed hopes; if running, disaster.

Automobile: Spiritual advancement. Note the speed at which the car is going.

Axe: Respect from others, though more for position than for abilities.

B

Baby/child: A sleeping child indicates a trusting nature. A crawling baby shows the need for making a quick decision. A crying baby symbolizes a number of small problems to be resolved.

Back door: An unexpected solution to a problem.

Badger: A sign of sagacity and wisdom.

Bagpipes: Help from an unexpected source.

Ball: Something difficult to hold onto.

Balloon: Seeming solid but in reality just full of air. A hot-air balloon rising symbolizes financial gain.

Banjo: A good time socially.

Barn: A store of what will be useful for the time ahead. A barn on fire means the loss of everything.

Basket: A full basket is a well-paying job; an empty basket is the loss of a job.

Bat: A bat flying around shows that a lot of small problems will be quickly cleared up. A bat hanging upside down means that what seem like small problems now will develop into big problems later.

Bear: Great hidden strength.

Bed: A place of security.

Bee: Profit; gain. A busy period.

Beehive: Success in business.

Bell: A single tolling bell signifies approaching death. A peal of bells is a celebration. A persistent doorbell is an alarm.

Bicycle: Spiritual advancement dependent upon effort put into it. It can also mean that things are becoming too mechanical and there is a need to become more creative.

Bird: Blackbird—caution.

Canary—sudden departure; sickness.

Crow—disappointment in what has been expected; having to make do with what is there.

Dove—love; happiness at home. Two doves together mean a reconciliation.

Eagle—great business success.

Hawk—business success; a swooping hawk is a legal success.

Lark—short vacation.

Nightingale—joyful news on its way; assured happiness.

Owl—a lot of thought will be needed for a coming problem; no snap decisions. To hear an owl hoot is warning of a coming problem.

Parrot—beware of slander; gossip.

Peacock—popularity; pride and vanity.

Pigeon—news coming in the form of a letter.

Raven—a family reunion.

Swallow—flying swallows mean happiness and good fortune. Nesting swallows mean close friendship.

Swan—happy and contented family life.

Vulture—a bitter enemy.

Bird's nest: A coming marriage.

Blacksmith: Success through hard work.

Boat/ship: A sailboat is complacency. If in stormy seas, then you are going to be busy. It can also be a more gentle form of spiritual progression. A steamship or motorboat shows steady progress with the ability to go faster.

Books: Spirit was greatly appreciated by people with whom spirit did business, as well as people spirit never actually met. To be reading a book is to have secrets revealed.

Bottle: A full bottle symbolizes the ability and the means to share with others. An empty bottle is a need, a yearning.

Bride: Wealth to come.

Bridge: To cross a bridge is to overcome difficulties.

Bucket: A full bucket means receiving something advantageous. An empty bucket is an opportunity to gain something.

Bull: A black or red bull indicates financial gain; a white bull is a gain in the field of love and friendship. To fight a bull means there is a need to concentrate all energy in one direction.

Burial/coffin: A need to end an episode. Tidy up loose ends and get ready for a completely new direction.

Butterfly: Flirting.

C

Camel: A succession of good things coming in. A long period of well-being.

Candle: Unlit, it is a symbol of opportunity. Lit, it is a revelation, a secret revealed.

Castle: Ambition.

Cat: A sleeping cat is an indication that there was a plot against spirit. A cat washing itself shows there had been a need to get organized. A walking or running cat was a missed opportunity.

Cave: An opportunity to go back and make a correction. Inside a cave is security.

Cemetery: Well-tended indicates many good and faithful friends. Unkempt means loss of friends and also indicates acquaintances rather than close friends.

Chain: Restriction.

Chess: Argument with family members. **Checkers** is an argument with others.

Church: Bad news on its way. Inside a church indicates depression and pessimism.

Circus: Indicates a very busy social and business calendar.

Coffin: If empty, this is a good sign, indicating long life and good health. A closed coffin indicates an early death.

Colors: Blue—need for a vacation.

>Brown—need to get to the root of a problem.

>Green—growth and abundance.

>Orange—new beginnings.

>Purple—richness and luxury.

>Red—danger and excitement.

>Yellow—happiness and family togetherness.

Corkscrew: An inquisitive friend who could cause problems.

Cow: A sign of home and comfort.

Crab: Possibility of a lawsuit with someone thought of as a friend.

Cradle: If a child is in it, then there is a child who will be prominent in your affairs. If the cradle is empty, then there will be a relocation.

Crocodile/alligator: An accident brought about by trying to avoid enemies.

Cross: An equal-armed cross is a sign of good luck. If enclosed in a circle, it is financial good luck.

Crossroads: A decision that will have far-reaching effects.

Crown: A warning.

D

Dagger: You will antagonize someone, or spirit antagonized someone.

Deer: Hard times ahead.

Dentist: Sudden change of fortune.

Desert: A search for knowledge.

Diamond: Social success. A necklace of diamonds indicates a long and happy marriage.

Dog: Running means a loss in a lawsuit. Being chased by a dog is the loss of a friend. To be bitten by a dog means an argument with your spouse. A barking dog is a sign of danger.

Dragon: A dangerous undertaking. Slaying a dragon is achieving success.

Drum: A sign of communication.

Duck/goose: When quacking, good news to come. When seen flying overhead, good news coming if flying from left to right; bad news if right to left.

E

Eggs: Much family love.

Elephant: Symbol of power.

Explosion: Fear of firm commitments. Possible lazy streak.

F

Falling: Need to escape from a situation.

Farm/farmer: Reward from hard work.

Faucet: If dripping, it indicates a waste of money being lost in small amounts. A running faucet is throwing away money. A faucet that is turned off shows caution in finances.

Feather: White indicates good luck; black is bad luck. A number of floating feathers is a chance to fulfill desires.

Fence: Restrictions. To climb over a fence is to seek to get out of a situation.

Fields: If overgrown, loss of control. If plowed, wonderful opportunity to plant seeds. If rich with harvest, you will have abundance.

Fire: A low, smoldering fire is suppressed desire. A blazing fire indicates things getting out of hand.

Fish: Swimming is a sign of joy and success. Eating a fish indicates the possibility of sickness.

Flying: Feeling of being restricted.

Forest: Peace and tranquility. If lost in a forest, it indicates family quarrels.

Fountain: A sign of love and a happy marriage.

Fox: Cleverness and cunning.

Frog: Progression by leaps and bounds.

Fruit: Apple—green indicates fickle friendships; red shows true friendship.

> Apricot—good health and contentment.
>
> Cherry—black cherries are deception, especially by a lover. Red shows complete trust.
>
> Grape—rejoicing, celebration.
>
> Lemon—struggle; someone with a sour disposition.

Melon—a journey across water.

Nut—conjugal happiness. To break open a nut means a struggle to get what is wanted, but when achieved it is well worthwhile.

Orange—amusement. Easily entertained.

Peach—a journey over land.

Pear—unexpected invitation to a party.

Plum—unchanging friendship; loyalty.

Strawberry—unexpected good fortune.

Funeral: Death of someone close. Unexpected inheritance.

G

Gate: Frustration if closed. If open, then smooth-running plans.

Giant: Insecurity.

Goat: Prosperity.

Gold: Tendency to greed. If you are buying gold, then you will lose friends because of this greed. If you are mining the gold, then you will overcome the tendency.

Golf: Long life, with opportunity to correct mistakes made.

Grasshopper: Coming financial losses.

Guitar: Happiness.

Gun: Arguments. Small guns—small arguments; big guns—big arguments.

Gypsy: A sign of future travel. A happy marriage. A group of gypsies indicates a reunion.

H

Hair: Short hair means unhappiness; long hair is happiness and good fortune. Disheveled hair means there are annoyances and arguments, while well-groomed hair means abundance. To cut your hair, or have it cut, means you may unknowingly be working against yourself and hurting yourself by your actions.

Hammer: Determination and force.

Hammock: A sign of selfishness and laziness.

Handcuffs: Your hands are tied.

Hearse: Since death is an end, and an end leads to a new beginning, a hearse symbolizes the start of a new job/career.

Hill: Climbing a hill is indicative of success in undertakings. Standing on top of a hill is security and power. Standing, looking up at a hill, is a challenge.

Horse: Good fortune. A black or brown horse is power and position; a white or grey horse is prosperity. A stallion is sexual power.

I

Insects: Restlessness. Need to relocate.

Intoxication: Need to guard against recklessness, especially reckless spending. To meet a drunk means beware of financial losses.

Ivy: Need for a medical check-up.

J

Jester: Embarrassment, for yourself or a close friend or relative.

Jockey: Many ideas but too little time in which to accomplish them.

Judge: To meet a judge indicates coming punishment.

Juggler: A very competitive nature.

K

Kettle: Domestic comfort.

Keys: You are capable, practical, and sensible.

Kite: Flying a kite shows you are not up to your job.

Knots: Tying knots means you are creating problems for yourself.

L

Ladder: Aspire to great things. Climbing a ladder means you will achieve them. Falling from a ladder indicates running afoul of the law.

Lamb: Inner peace and happiness.

Letter(s): A discovery that is beneficial. An opportunity to better yourself.

Lightning: Trouble brought about by a woman you have been close to. Lightning striking a tree or building indicates a court case brought about by a woman.

Lion: Lasting friendship. Strength; leadership.

Lock: Entering something forbidden. Care should be taken.

Locket: Long-term friendship; affectionate relationship. Joy and happiness.

Locomotive: Ability to do anything you wish. Powerful spiritual development.

M

Magistrate: An error made, of which you were unaware.

Maid: Good news is on its way.

Mail carrier: Negotiations with a salesperson. Possible overcharging.

Mandolin: An intimate, romantic time.

Marionettes: Manipulation.

Mattress: Any present problems will disappear and you will be comfortable again.

Maypole: A sign of being in love.

Medals: Recognition for some achievement.

Mermaid: Great expectations, followed by big disappointments.

Mirror: Betrayal by a friend.

Moon: Full moon means you will be blessed. New moon means a wish will be granted. Partially clouded moon means luck in love. A moon reflected in water means great expectations but disappointment in love.

Mountain: Lofty aspirations.

Mouse: Small, petty annoyances.

N

Necklace: To be wearing a fine necklace indicates taking part in an important social event. A small, insignificant necklace can be petty jealousies and annoyances.

Newspaper: Buying a newspaper means you will receive a letter. Reading a newspaper means receipt of news that could be good or bad.

Numbers: Zero—harmony; unity.

> One—solitude; loneliness.

> Two—happiness; the perfect couple.

> Three—arguments; disputes.

> Four—choices; decisions.

> Five—balance.

> Six—exploration; being outgoing.

> Seven—good luck and many blessings.

> Eight—new beginnings.

> Nine—family and children.

Nurse: You are tired of responsibility. You need assistance.

O

Oak tree: A good, solid marriage.

Oar: Rowing with a pair of oars shows forging ahead by your own efforts. Losing an oar means you have made a mistake that will slow you down.

Onion: There are many layers to what is happening around you, so don't jump to conclusions.

Organ: To hear organ music means good news is coming. It will be bad news if the chords are discordant.

Oxen: Great inner strength, but despite hard work there will be little progress.

ℙ

Palace: Raising your standards of living. Beware of living beyond your means.

Palm tree: Honor and victory. There will be recognition of what you have achieved.

Parasol: Many good, close friends.

Pawnshop: Exchanging one set of problems for another set.

Pen/pencil: Being in a position to make a choice affecting many people.

Piano: A piano being played indicates an invitation to a party. If you are playing the piano, then you will be giving the party.

Picnic: A good time with close friends.

Pig: Assured success. Good time for investing.

Pine tree: An exciting and possibly dangerous exploit.

Pirate: A lot of traveling, but be careful of accidents.

Pistol/revolver: An explosive temper. Be careful of what is said and what is done.

Pitchfork: A sign of excellent health.

Plow: Concentrate on doing your best. What you do now will be judged in the future.

Police: An action of yours will need to be explained to your friends and acquaintances.

Pope: Indication of extravagance; over-spending.

Q

Queen: Coming prosperity.

Quilt: Financial advances. Also, gossip and flattery.

R

Rabbit: A chance to increase prosperity. A black rabbit is a sign of high-risk finances; a white one is a sign of a legacy.

Railroad: Slow but steady progress with security in the long run.

Rat: A secret enemy working against you, in the sense of learning your secrets to use to their own advantage. Someone seeming to be a friend is actually an enemy.

Reptile: Someone you are not sure about is actually a good friend.

Ring: A cheap and flashy ring indicates a minor ailment. A rich, expensive ring shows robust, excellent health.

River: With smooth waters indicates happiness and success; with rough and/or muddy waters indicates a risky journey that could lead to success.

Road: Wide and straight means things will go along easily and effortlessly; winding and hilly means a difficult and tiring journey.

Rocking chair: An easy and contented life.

S

Saddle: Ease and comfort in life.

Sailor: Indicative of journeys. Possibly much relocating.

Sand: An increase in finances. Good return on investments.

Scissors: Enemies. Misfortune.

Shadows: Pessimism and the possibility of failure.

Shamrock: A wonderful time with someone very much admired.

Shark: Danger from jealous enemies.

Sheep: Slow and steady progress.

Shipwreck: A dangerous illness but not fatal.

Shirt: To take off a shirt means to lose a friend. To lose a button off a shirt means petty squabbles. To wear a bright, clean shirt means happiness on its way.

Silver: Honors and prestige.

Singing: Meeting old friends. Singing solo means finding yourself alone.

Skeleton: Involvement in some unusual activity. If the skeleton carries a scythe, then there will be cutting back and pruning taking place.

Skull: A big discovery that will be beneficial.

Smoke: A brief moment of joy, but it will not last. To smoke a cigarette, cigar, or pipe indicates great self-confidence that may not be justified.

Snail: Slow and steady progress, but be sure you are going in the right direction.

Snow: Light snow is a sign of contentment; heavy snow is a warning to be careful.

Soldier: Trouble to come.

Spider: Luck and great prosperity. If the spider is on a web, then the prosperity will come from a number of different sources.

Stag: Financial gain.

Stars: Recovery from an illness. A shooting star signifies the birth of a child.

Steamboat: Unexpected news from afar.

Sunrise/sunset: Success in a new venture.

Sword: Recognition and reward.

T

Tailor: You will be very busy with little time to enjoy yourself.

Tambourine: You will be held accountable for your actions.

Tattoo: Inability to keep a secret.

Tears: Receipt of a letter bearing bad news.

Tent: Temporary security.

Tiger: Fierce enmity. Animosity toward a particular person.

Toad: The possibility of an accident.

Trumpet: A mild flirtation that could develop into something serious if allowed to.

Tunnel: Success in negotiating through difficult times, especially in business.

Turkey: Invitation to make a speech.

U

Umbrella: Feelings of vulnerability. Need for protection. An open umbrella is a stronger indicator than a closed one.

Undertaker: A coming death, though no one related to you.

V

Valley: A sign of contentment and tranquility. A knowledge of protection.

Vault: A bank vault is a sign of hidden riches. You are trying to attain something, but being frustrated.

Venus: A search for the ideal woman.

Violin: Symbolizes good company and enjoyment. If you are playing the violin, then you are much admired and loved.

W

Wasp: Trouble from envious people. To be stung by a wasp means that you are spending money foolishly.

Watch: A visit from a very important person.

Waterfall: You will meet many new and interesting people.

Wedding: New friends.

Whirlpool: You are in a very dangerous situation and could lose control at any minute.

Windmill: An inheritance. If the sails are turning, it will be large; if still, it will be small.

Wolf: Strength and independence.

Worm: There may be contact with someone who has a contagious disease.

Y

Yacht: You will become friendly with someone who is very wealthy. If you are sailing the yacht, then it is you who will become wealthy.

Yew tree: A symbol of strength yet flexibility.

Z

Zebra: A misplaced friendship.

Zodiac: Indicates great interest in your fellow humans. You have an inquiring and active mind.

Remember: These interpretations may apply to you or they may apply to spirit, bringing affirmation that it *is* spirit in contact with you.

Table-Tipping

Table Tipping

Table-tipping—sometimes called table "turning"—was one of the very earliest methods of communicating with spirit. Shortly after the initial "rap session" that the Fox sisters had with the spirit of the peddler Charles B. Rosna, they moved on to table-tipping as a much faster and more accurate method. Nandor Fodor, author and psychic-science investigator, described table-tipping as "the crudest form of communication with the subconscious self or with extraneous intelligences."[6] Crude or not, tables have been used for hundreds of years—if not for spirit communication, then certainly for divination.

Tables are usually used by a group of people. They sit around with fingertips resting lightly on the outer edge of the top surface. The spokesperson for the group will then call out to spirit, trying to make contact. When contact *is* established, the table will rock up onto one or two of its legs and then drop back down onto the ground again. A code is established for the number of such thumps for *yes* and the number for *no* so that questions may be asked.

Working alone, it is recommended that you use a three-legged table, though four legs will work fine. It's

6. Fodor, *Encyclopedia of Psychic Science*, 374.

said that an all-wood table is best, one with no metal in-corporated into it. In other words, the legs should either be glued into the top or wooden pegs should be used rather than screws or nails. If you truly believe that this will make a difference, then go with it. However, many people believe that it makes no difference whether or not there is metal contained in the table—some have even worked with an all-metal table. It's what you yourself be-lieve that matters.

With the three-legged table, sit with the two legs—one on either side of your own legs. With your fingers resting on the surface in front of you, this arrangement will then facilitate the table tipping toward you. When you begin, make the statement to spirit that tipping the table toward you constitutes *yes* and tipping it away from you (to either side) constitutes *no* as an answer to any question asked.

In order to get full messages, ask spirit to tip up the table on two of its legs (it doesn't really matter which two) and to drop back down when you call out the cor-rect letter of the alphabet. For example, if the answer to a question, coming from spirit, is "daytime," then the table will remain poised on its two legs while you call out "A—B—C—D . . ." At "D" it will drop down to indicate that letter. The next time it would drop would be when you call "A" and then when you go to "Y," and so on.

Start your table-tipping session with a meditation, building the white light, and then proceed to a gentle singing of something melodic and light. You may prefer to simply hum. If you play an instrument, then utilize that, playing for a few moments before laying down the instrument and placing your fingers on the table. Pray if you feel the need to. Study the photograph or artifact of the spirit you want to contact and then relax and call on him or her to join you. State: "If you are here, would you please tip the table? Thank you." Keep speaking like this until the table does tip—which it will do.

Make a list of questions beforehand, as many as possible that can be answered either *yes* or *no*. This will be more rewarding, in many ways, than having the spirit try to spell out long messages. If a message, or a name, is being spelled out and you think you know what is being attempted, don't hesitate to ask. For example, if spirit spells out "M-I-C-H . . ." you can shout out "Michael?" If you are right, then the table will give the thump for *yes* and you will have saved some time and energy. Again, keep a careful record of what you receive. A tape recorder can help here, but be sure to transcribe the results as soon as possible after the session.

Occasionally the table will rock up onto two legs and then go on to balance on just one leg. From there it will many times start to rotate (hence the term "table turning"), and you will have to get out of your seat and run around trying to keep up with it. This can be a very strong indication of spirit communication. (I have even been at a séance where the table has "walked" across the room and stopped at a bookcase, when it needed to refer to a specific title. Don't be surprised at anything spirit does!)

Do keep your fingers on the top edge of the table and try not to apply too much pressure. It is, after all, spirit who will use your muscles to cause the table to tip. Don't fight any tendency for the table to tilt but don't try to direct the tipping yourself.

Automatic Writing/ Drawing/ Painting/Doodling

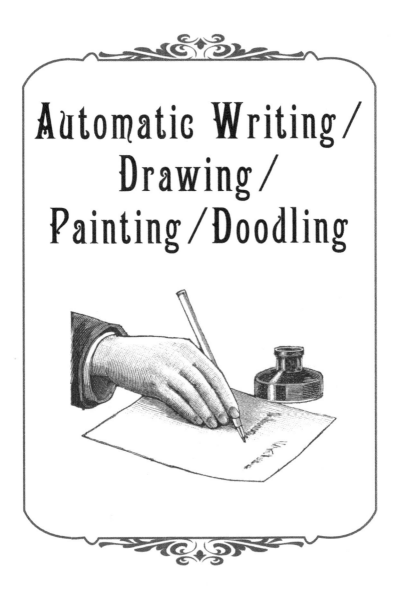

o you doodle? Consciously or unconsciously? To doodle consciously is to be thinking about what you are doing (though probably not with all of your concentration, since you usually doodle when on the phone or talking to someone). For example, you might scribble the outline of a flower, then go on to add petals, and then more flowers, and then to make it into a bouquet . . . that sort of thing. But to doodle unconsciously is when you are caught up in your conversation, or whatever the activity, to the point that you are scribbling on a piece of paper without looking at it and have no idea what you are drawing until you finally look down when the conversation ends. It's this unconscious doodling that ties in with spirit communication, and is frequently guided by spirit.

When you find that you have doodled without thinking about it, closely examine the scribbling. Turn the paper around and view it from all directions. See if you can make out any letters, numbers, or symbols. Occasionally, even though you have not been paying attention to what your hand was writing, you will find that you have written someone's name, a number or series of numbers, or have drawn a recognizable sign or symbol. If you know you are going to doodle, it's a good idea to have a large piece of paper available so that—as can happen—if spirit has a long message to deliver to you, then there is the opportunity to do so. Yes, what starts as a doodle can develop (again unconsciously) into a lengthy message from spirit.

The problem is that when you become aware of the fact that your hand is doodling, is scribbling on the paper, then it is human nature to look and see what you are producing. Fight this temptation. If you suddenly become aware that you are doodling, then keep your focus on the conversation, or whatever, and make a point of *not* looking or trying to sense what your hand is doing.

Spirit frequently wants to make contact with you. One of the most satisfactory methods is with the written word. Spirit will take control of your hand and arm and will direct them to produce a written "letter" to you. A more formalized version of this is done with automatic writing, which we will look at in a moment.

The doodle is the most basic form of automatic writing and drawing. In itself, it can be a wonderful way of communicating with spirit. At least it can be a great introduction to the more detailed automatic writing and/or drawing.

If you are going to set out to do automatic writing, then prepare ahead of time by getting as large a piece of paper as possible. It's possible to work with just a simple writing pad, but most automatic writing becomes extensive and if you can keep from having to turn pages, you will be better able to preserve the flow of the communication. I often suggest getting an old roll of wallpaper and using the back of it. It's also possible to get leftover cutoffs from printing runs at newspaper offices. Even large rolls of wrapping paper will suffice.

Sit comfortably at a table, which may be in front of you or to one side. Hold a pen or pencil in your hand and let your hand rest lightly on the paper. Then focus your attention on something else. That "something else" can be reading a book, talking on the phone, watching television, talking to a friend who is with you, or anything similar—anything that will hold your attention for a period of time so that you don't have to look down at what your hand is doing on the paper.

Beforehand, as with other exercises given in this book, you can invite spirit to make contact. Go through your meditation and white-light building, ending with an invitation to spirit to make contact. Then forget all about automatic writing and get into your conversation, reading, or television watching. Ignore your hand. But after a relatively short while, you may notice that your hand starts to move of its own volition. It will feel like a nervous movement; your hand will start to scribble rapidly on the paper. Continue to ignore it, and it will continue scribbling.

What happens is that the scribbling slowly changes from a rapid (and it can be extremely rapid) up and down movement into a swirling: the making of loops and circles. This, in turn, will gradually give way to loops and swirls similar to writing. Then again, in turn, this will become actual writing: actual letters formed and written very, very fast. When this has been going on for some considerable time, take the opportunity to break your attention and focus and look at the paper. You will be surprised to find that your hand has written words. They may not be easy to make out at first, but the more you continue with the experiment, the clearer will the writing become.

Usually the writing is nothing like your own handwriting. You may possibly recognize it as the hand of a deceased loved one—the spirit making contact. There are even records of the writing coming through in a foreign language, one with which the writer was not familiar. There have also been records of an automatic writer producing two different documents at the same time, in two different handwritings: one from the left hand and one from the right. It's unlikely that you'll do that in the early stages of experimenting, though don't rule out anything!

It can also be that, rather than producing writing, spirit comes through to draw or even paint (if you have the materials available). Some communicators who could never draw anything, by their own admission, have produced wonderful drawings and paintings directed by spirit.

Automatic writing is one of the more immediate forms of spirit communication, in that, once it has been established—in other words, once you have accepted that spirit is in command and it is not you who are controlling what is written—you can begin to have a "conversation" with spirit, asking questions and receiving the written answers. Long conversations and discussions have been recorded in this way.

In the past, Jane Roberts received many of the teachings of "Seth" through automatic writing. Also, the majority of the multi-volume works of Patience Worth were received by Pearl Curran through automatic writing. There were approximately 2,500 poems, short stories, plays, and allegories, as well as six full-length novels, authored by that spirit!

Planchette

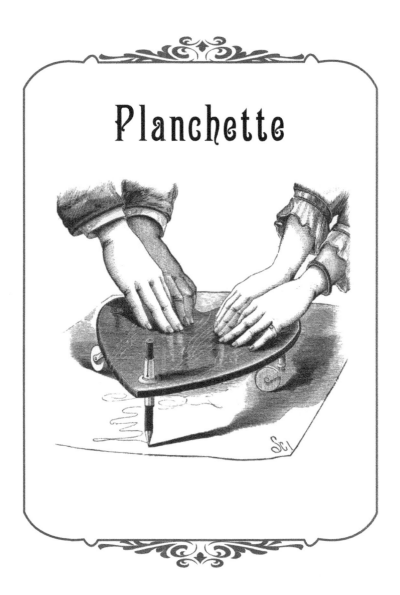

The word *planchette* means "plank, small board, or platform." It's applied to a small moving platform used to communicate with spirits. A form of it is found with the Ouija® board.

The planchette is generally heart-shaped, or it can be circular. It rests on three supports—two of them are castors or small wheels (or maybe tipped with felt so that they glide easily over a paper surface), and the third is the point of a pencil or pen. This writing instrument goes through a hole in the planchette so that it protrudes underneath to align with the two wheels. If the planchette rests on a sheet of paper, then as it is moved about the paper, the pen-point leaves a line. With the fingertips of the operator resting lightly on the edge of the planchette (much as on the edge of the table used for table-tipping), spirit can use the person's muscles to direct the pen and produce writing.

The apparatus was invented in 1853 by a Frenchman and was quickly adopted by Spiritualists around the world. It's applied to a small moving platform used to communicate with spirits. (Another form of it is found on the Ouija® board, which I'll discuss later.)

Start as with the earlier exercises: breathing, meditation, white light, invitation to spirit. Then focus your attention on the planchette and ask spirit to communicate. Ask that it write on the paper, using the planchette. You will find that with practice and perseverance the planchette will, in fact, start to move. Usually it moves around and around the paper, getting faster and faster. This is spirit "getting the feel" of your muscles and of the energy available. It will then settle down and you can ask it questions. Rest the tips of the fingers of both hands on the rim of the planchette, to give spirit as much energy as possible. The answers to the questions will be written out, either fully or in symbolic form. Sometimes a picture will be drawn rather than a sentence spelled out. Sometimes, too, initials will be written rather than full names.

Initially (as with doodles), you may have to study what seems like a mess of scribbling in order to find anything at all that seems relevant. The more you use the planchette, however, the more used to it will spirit become until good, immediately readable information is provided. So be patient. But, as I say, *whatever* comes through will be significant—it may just need sorting and recognizing.

On occasion, spirit will use the planchette to produce art, the scribbling rapidly becoming shading and hatching to produce a drawing. It may be a sketch of the spirit himself or herself, or it may be something pertinent to the contact—like a scene where spirit used to live, for example. There are endless possibilities as to what may be produced.

Talking Boards/ Ouija®

The name *Ouija* is taken from the French *oui* and the German *ja*, both meaning "yes." Variations on the popular board have been around for centuries. In ancient Greece there was a small table used that moved about and pointed to letters of the alphabet, spelling out messages from the gods. Circa 550 BCE, in China, a similar tool was popular.

In ancient Rome there was a form of divination termed *alectromancy* or *alectryomancy*—a name that comes from the Greek *alectruon*, meaning "rooster," and *manteia*, meaning "divination." As the name suggests, it utilized the actions of a cockerel or a hen. It was often used in Rome to identify robbers and had to be done when either the sun or the moon was in Aries or Leo. The letters of the alphabet were scratched into the dirt in a large circle and a small pile of grain was placed at each letter. An all-white rooster was placed in the center of the circle, a question was asked, and the officiating priest would note the letters from which the bird pecked the grain. These letters would spell out the answer to the question.

The modern talking board is a large, flat board with the letters of the alphabet written on it, usually in a wide semi-circle though sometimes in a full circle. A small platform on wheels is placed in the center of the board. This platform, or planchette, is often heart-shaped so that there is a point that can indicate a letter as the planchette moves about the board. The operator rests his or her fingertips on the edge of the planchette and addresses spirit, to ask questions. The planchette will move about the board, guided by spirit, pointing to letters to spell out the answer.

The first commercially produced board was patented in the late 1800s by Elijah J. Bond, who, in 1892, sold the patent to William Fuld, founder of the Southern Novelty Company in Maryland. Fuld produced the board under the name "Oriole Talking Board," later labeled "Ouija, the Mystifying Oracle." In 1966, Parker Brothers bought the rights and marketed the board to the point that it even outsold the previously most popular game, Monopoly.

There are some minor problems with the design of the Ouija® board, which have been overcome in my own design, "The Buckland Spirit Board" (see also my 2006 book *Ouija—"Yes! Yes!"*). For example, there can be confusion as to exactly which letter is being indicated because, as well as the pointed end of the planchette, the Fuld board has a "window" that is supposed to center over the chosen letter. But sometimes when you think a letter is indicated by the window, spirit is actually using the point of the planchette to indicate a letter on the line above! This

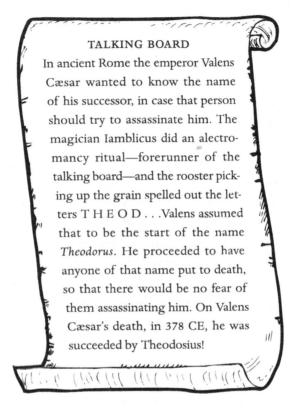

TALKING BOARD

In ancient Rome the emperor Valens Cæsar wanted to know the name of his successor, in case that person should try to assassinate him. The magician Iamblicus did an alectromancy ritual—forerunner of the talking board—and the rooster picking up the grain spelled out the letters T H E O D . . . Valens assumed that to be the start of the name *Theodorus*. He proceeded to have anyone of that name put to death, so that there would be no fear of them assassinating him. On Valens Cæsar's death, in 378 CE, he was succeeded by Theodosius!

can be overcome by putting masking tape over the window and going just with the pointing of the planchette. There is also a tendency for the planchette to get "hung up" when one of the planchette's legs slips over the edge of the board while moving to a letter at the end of a line. All you can do is to lift it back on again.

Although a board can be operated by as many as six or so people simultaneously, it is more frequently used by just two but can equally well be used by only one, for a solitary séance.

Do your usual preparatory work and then sit quietly with the board in front of you. Before you place your fingers on the planchette, form in your mind the image of the spirit you wish to address. Having a photograph of that person nearby is a help. Call upon this person (aloud or silently) to be present and to answer your questions. Then place your fingertips lightly on the edge of the planchette and ask, aloud, "Is there anybody there?" It will very quickly move to the word *Yes* on the board. After each answer, the planchette should return to the center of the board. If it does not, then simply ask it to do so.

If the planchette just sits there, without moving . . . have patience. It many times takes a while for spirit to adjust to controlling your muscles. However, if you have tried a number of times, on a variety of occasions, and still the board refuses to move, then gently move it yourself, by pressure of your fingers, to go around the board in a clockwise circle a number of times. Do this and then stop and see if spirit can now take over. This usually does the trick in getting things moving. Once spirit does take command, then don't try to direct it yourself.

It can get a little confusing when the planchette spells out a long message. To make it easier to understand, ask spirit to move around in a complete circle at the end of each word. If any word is unclear, don't hesitate to ask spirit to spell it again. To repeat what I say in my book *The Fortune-Telling Book:*[7]

> *Many times what is recorded seems to make little sense at first. It appears that this is not an easy method of communicating from the next world back to this one. There is often confusion between similar-looking letters: N, M, and H; O and Q; P and R; I and J, and so on. Careful study of the written results should make it possible to correct any such substitutions . . . Other possible problems might be receiving anagrams, or finding letters arranged as though by a person with dyslexia.*

Despite the various "horror stories" that have become urban legends (that talking boards can lead to possession, for example!), this is an excellent way of communicating with spirit. Just remember that "like attracts like" and that it is *extremely* unlikely that you will encounter a hostile spirit. If you do . . . hang up the phone!

---

7. p. 356.

Inspirational
Writing

After doing the preliminaries of meditating, white-light building, singing, and calling upon spirit, sit with a large writing pad in front of you and a pen or pencil in your hand. With automatic writing you leave it to spirit to do the actual writing—the moving of the pen on the paper—but with inspirational writing it is *you* who will do the composition. The difference is that spirit will *inspire* you . . . hence, "inspirational" writing. In effect, spirit will dictate to you.

It is as though you can hear the words in your head, and all you have to do is to put them down on paper. There have been whole books written in this way . . . my own *Buckland's Domino Divination*—a new form of divination using those tiles—came to me in this form. Inspirational art and even inspirational speaking are forms of this spirit communication.

It is not easy to recognize when it is spirit that is telling you what to write and when it is your own conscious mind. If you find that you have to think hard about what you are trying to say, if you keep rephrasing things or stumbling over words, then it is probably your conscious mind that is constructing what you are writing. Inspirational writing by its very definition flows easily and without effort.

You, as the medium for this form of spirit expression, enter into a light trance. Wolfgang Amadeus Mozart said, "When all goes well with me, when I am in a carriage, or walking, or when I cannot sleep at night, the thoughts come streaming in upon me most fluently; whence or how is more than I can tell." Many musicians, as well as artists and writers, have had this same experience.

There have been many books written through inspirational writing; those of William Stainton Moses are especially notable. More recently there is a series of nine books under the heading *Conversations with God*, by Neale Donald Walsch.

Rosemary Brown claimed that dead composers dictated new musical compositions to her. She created a small media sensation in the 1970s by claiming to produce new works by Johann Sebastian Bach, Ludwig van Beethoven, Johannes Brahms, Frédéric Chopin, Claude Debussy, Edvard Grieg, Franz Liszt, Sergei Rachmaninoff, Franz Schubert, and Robert Schumann. A number of notable musicians were impressed (including André Previn and Virgil Thomson), while others said the new compositions lacked the spark of the composers' earlier works.

Pendulum

Using the pendulum is known as *radiesthesia*—also *rhabdomancy*, or *cleidomancy*. One of the best-known uses of the pendulum is in dowsing, in finding where to drill for water. But it is also used for many other things, not least of all for communicating with spirit.

The pendulum is, as its name implies, a weight hanging from a method of suspension. For the purposes of working with spirit, it is on the end of a fine chain or a length of ribbon or thread. The length of the chain should be about six to ten inches. The weight can be any one of a number of things. There are pendulums sold for this purpose that are usually semi-precious stones or crystals on fine chains, with a small bead to hold at the other end of the chain. These are ideal. You can also simply take off a ring from your finger and hang it from a piece of thread or a ribbon. Or you can use a pendant from around your neck. You can use any one of a number of things. It doesn't matter what the weight is made of; it can be a stone, as mentioned, or plastic, brass, steel, silver, gold . . . the choice is yours.

Sit at a table and hold the end of the chain between your thumb and first finger. You can use either hand.

Some people say that your elbow must not rest on the table, but I find it makes no difference. In fact, if you *don't* rest your elbow, then your arm can get tired after a long session. Let the pendulum hang down so that the weight is just off the surface of the table. Try to keep the pendulum still, so that it's not swinging.

You are going to be asking questions of spirit, and the pendulum will then swing to indicate the answers. It is important that you don't consciously make the pendulum swing, since you want spirit to be in charge. It helps if most of your questions are in the form that will give *yes* or *no* answers. In fact, it is best to try to phrase your questions for this, so that you can get through a lot of information in a relatively short time.

First, then, you need to establish what represents *yes* and what represents *no*. I usually find that the pendulum swinging toward me and away from me is *yes* and swinging across me is *no*. But some people find the reverse of that is true, while still others find that it swings in a circle . . . clockwise for *yes* and counterclockwise for *no*. The only way to find out is to ask spirit.

So, sit comfortably at the table, invite spirit to join you, and then ask spirit to swing the pendulum to show *yes*. Immediately, or after a moment or two, the pendulum will swing. Make a note of the direction. Then ask

PENDULUM

In the 1920s there was a Swedish medium—Anna Rasmussen—who worked with the pendulum, and with her spirit guide, Dr. Lazarus. Spirit first worked with Anna when Anna was only twelve years old. In later years she was thoroughly examined and intensely tested by a Professor Winther in Copenhagen. The professor designed a sealed glass case with a number of pendulums inside, hanging from silk threads. By simply concentrating on whichever pendulum the professor indicated, Anna was able to get it to swing, even though she had no direct contact with it. Dr. Lazarus's spirit then directed the swing to answer the professor's questions.

spirit to stop the swinging. When it comes to rest, ask it to swing to represent *no*, and again make note of that and ask spirit to stop.

You can build up several common phrases. For example, as I've said, I use a swing to and fro for *yes*, and across for *no*. I then have spirit swing it in a clockwise circle for "Rephrase the question" and in a counterclockwise circle for "Cannot answer that question." The rephrasing is because we sometimes will ask something that is ambiguous or that cannot be easily answered with a yes or no, so here spirit asks that I put the question a different way. That has been useful many times.

You can work with the same sort of questions that you would use for any of the other forms of spirit communication, be it talking board, automatic writing, planchette, or anything. If you need spirit to give you a full message, then there are one or two ways of going about it. The first is to let the pendulum hang down inside a wine glass or tumbler and then to call out the letters of the alphabet. The pendulum will swing out and strike the side of the glass when you reach the letter that spirit intends. It's not easy for spirit to get the pendulum swinging suddenly or to necessarily give a good sound as it strikes the glass, so call out the letters with plenty of time/space between them and ask spirit to strike the glass two or three times at the designated letter. This way there can be no mistake and no "accidental" clinking of the glass.

A second method is to make up a card, or sheet of paper, with the letters of the alphabet arranged in a circle, much as on a talking board. Mark a cross in the very center and hold the pendulum so that it hangs down over that central cross. This time the pendulum will swing out over the intended letter, but again give it time. It would not be easy to quickly change direction, so ask spirit to swing at least three times over the letter. You will find, then, that it will swing several times over one letter and then swing backward and forward over others as it moves around the circle until it arrives at the next needed letter, and then it will start swinging several times over that one, and so on.

You can get other information from spirit. For example, if you are trying to locate somebody or something, you can work with a map. Hold the pendulum with one hand, and with the other hand point your finger at the map. You can trace a route on the map, asking spirit for *yes* or *no* indications of which way to go, whether to turn left or right, what to do at a crossroads, and so forth. There is a wealth of information you can get from spirit when working with a pendulum.

Skrying

Skrying (sometimes spelled *scrying*) is the general name for things such as crystal-gazing, mirror-gazing, working with a speculum or polished copper surface, and so on. In other words, it is working with any reflective surface. Depicted in the frescoes painted around the walls of the Initiation Room at the Villa of Mysteries, in Pompeii, Italy, is a scene of an Initiate gazing into a polished copper bowl. Behind the Initiate a priest is holding up a mask representing Dionysus. When the Initiate sees that mask reflected in the bowl, it triggers an association with the god, which in turn leads to what is known as *palingenesis*: a rebirth by reliving the death and resurrection of the deity.

Queen Elizabeth I's astrologer was Dr. John Dee, who used what was termed a *shew-stone* (show stone). It was a flattened piece of dark glass that worked like a crystal ball, allowing Dr. Dee—or his assistant Edward Kelley— to see visions in the reflective surface. In fact, Kelley referred to the images he saw as "angels." These "angels" were in fact spirits, and skrying is a common method of communicating with them.

A good crystal ball can be very expensive. By a "good" crystal ball, I mean one that has no scratches, blemishes, or marks of any kind in it or on it. Glass balls are often used, being less expensive, but they may well have tiny bubbles inside them. Plastic balls are readily available, but they scratch very easily. The trouble with any sort of blemish is that when trying to gaze into the ball, the eye is automatically drawn to the bubble, scratch, or whatever. This defeats the purpose, which is to "lose yourself" in the ball's interior.

I'll first detail how to use a crystal and then I'll explain how you can use other less expensive items to get the same results.

You need to be in a totally quiet environment. As with all of the other experiments in this book, sit quietly and go through your meditation and white-light building, ending with an invitation to spirit to make contact. If there is one particular spirit you would like to contact, then concentrate on him or her for a short period but then put them out of your mind. Have the crystal ball on a table in front of you, resting on a piece of black cloth (velvet is best). This way, as you gaze at the ball your mind will not be distracted by anything around it. Sit comfortably, with your back straight. If you are sitting in a chair, then have your feet flat on the ground and do not cross your legs. You can, however, sit cross-legged on the floor and rest the cloth and crystal on your lap or hold it in the palm of your hand.

You should have low light, and I would recommend a single candle, placed behind you so that you won't see it reflected in the crystal.

Gaze into the crystal, focusing on the very center of it. Be relaxed but not rigidly so—in other words, there's no need to keep your eyes locked open, unblinking! You can blink quite normally if you need to. Don't try to imagine anything in the ball. It's not easy to keep your mind clear but try to, so that you are not simply imagining pictures in the crystal. Breathe normally.

Many people see what looks like a mist or smoke slowly filling the crystal as they gaze into it. It gets denser and denser and then reverses and slowly thins out. When it thins, it reveals a picture. It can be a still picture or a moving one, in black and white or in color. It's almost like looking at a miniature television picture. For some people the picture comes without the smoke. It can take from two to ten minutes for this to happen. In fact, it might not happen at all the first time you try it, but don't be discouraged; keep trying. I wouldn't recommend trying for more than about ten minutes at a time. If it doesn't work, then try again another day and keep on at different times until it does work.

> **SKRYING**
> A drawing by Leonardo da Vinci, which is now in the library of Christ Church, in Oxford, England, shows a woman holding up a mirror to a seeress so that she may skry as part of a ritual. In the mirror can be seen the face of an old man.

Look carefully at what appears. Many times what does appear is a symbol. It's a good idea to familiarize yourself with the symbology found in dream interpretation (see the chapter in this book on dreams), for that can also apply to what appears in skrying. Look especially for numbers and initials.

A mirror can work just as well as a crystal ball, but make sure that it is angled so that you can't see anything specific reflected in it. Perhaps angle it so that it shows you the white ceiling or a plain wall. Better than a regular mirror is a black mirror. Get a photo frame and take out the glass. Paint one side of the glass black. Replace the glass with the painted surface to the rear, so that it's the black shiny side you see. Then set up that and proceed as previously suggested.

You can also use a tumbler of water. Fill the glass to the brim and stand it on a piece of black cloth on the table in front of you. Gaze down into it as with the crystal. You should not, of course, use a glass that has any painted design or similar on its sides; a plain clear glass is what you want.

Keep records of what you see. Many times you will see something that doesn't seem especially important, but when you review your notes days or weeks later, it suddenly becomes significant. Always keep notes of all your experiments. Once you've got the hang of skrying, you'll find that virtually any reflective surface can trigger a connection.

Tarot

The tarot is only one of many decks you can use. Though generally associated with psychic readings, the cards can also be used for communicating with spirit. Doing a tarot-card séance involves laying out chosen cards in a particular traditional pattern and then studying the symbols on those cards, based on their positions, and recognizing their significance with regard to the departed loved one.

First of all, you need one card to represent spirit . . . the particular spirit you want to connect with. I'll term this the *Spirit Card*. You can find this by looking through *all* of the cards. Have a picture in your mind of him or her, and then fairly quickly run through the deck looking for a card that would seem to be a good one to represent this spirit. It may be that the figure depicted in the artwork on the card reminds you of him or her, or it may just be a strong sensation or feeling that whatever is shown on the card is a connection. You have seventy-eight cards to choose from, so you should be able to find one that "feels right." If you just can't decide, then you can use one of the court cards. Use a king or queen for an older person, a knight for a younger man, and a page for a younger woman. Use either a sword or wand suit for someone who was dark-haired and a pentacle or cups suit for someone who was fair-haired. Take that card and set it aside.

However, an alternate and more precise (and, to my mind, much better) method is to not use a card at all but to substitute a photograph of the deceased. Place this where the Spirit Card would normally be.

Shuffle the rest of the cards and then cut them with your left hand, to the left. Spread all the cards, *face down*, across the table and pull out ten cards placing them, still face down, in a pile. These are the ones you will use for the séance. There are various layouts that can be used, but for the sake of explaining the process I'll stick with one of the most popular layouts: the Celtic Cross. The layout for the Celtic Cross is as follows:

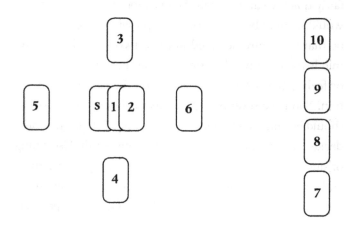

S is the spirit's photograph (or the Spirit Card you chose first) and is laid down in the center, *face up*. It is then covered by the first of the ten cards chosen, which is laid on it *face down* (all the remaining cards are laid face down). The second card chosen is laid across those two. The third card is placed above these and the fourth below them. The fifth is placed to the left and the sixth to the right. The remaining (7 through 10) are laid down in a vertical line to the right of these in ascending order.

The meanings of these various positions are as follows: **1**—that which covers spirit; **2**—that which crosses spirit; **3**—what is above; **4**—what is below; **5**—what is behind (in the past); **6**—what lies ahead; **7**—spirit himself/herself; **8**—spirit's "house"; **9**—hopes and fears; **10**—final outcome.

That which covers spirit: (**1**) is the impression that spirit created (I'll talk more about the individual card interpretations in a moment). For example, you might have seen your Uncle Charles as an easygoing, lovable guy, but the card that covers him shows him as a powerful king. However, when he was alive you only knew him in the family environment. Questioning family members and business acquaintances confirms that, as a businessman, Charles was indeed very purposeful and powerful.

What crosses him: (2) shows the forces or people who worked against him and, again, with a little research you will probably find that what is indicated by the card was, in fact, what he had to struggle and contend with.

It is spirit that is directing these cards. Spirit directed you to pick out these particular ten cards, because they are the ones that will give you the true, detailed picture of your loved one. The purpose of Spiritualism is to prove the continuity of life after the transition we term death. This is exactly what is happening here. By controlling the selection of the cards, spirit is providing the information that proves the contact with this particular spirit.

What is above: (3) relates to what he or she really aspired to. Although a business tycoon in everyday life, it might be that Uncle Charles really aspired to a life where he could "stop and smell the roses"; perhaps he had a secret longing to write poetry!

What is below: (4) is that which he felt deep down inside. In fact, this may well also reflect what he aspired to, or perhaps it will show that he had a tremendous inferiority complex. There are several cross-checks with this layout, several cards that confirm others. For example, if you are using a card as the Spirit Card, rather than a photograph, then *you* chose that card. You may then find that much of what you had seen when you chose that card is also reflected in cards **1**, **3,** and **7**, provided by spirit. Similarly, what is shown as crossing him (**2**) may well be reflected in hopes and fears (**9**). His "house" (**8**) relates to his close friends and/or family, so this may well correlate with several of the other cards.

What is behind: (**5**) deals with spirit's early life.

What is ahead: (**6**) relates to any legacy that spirit may leave, anything for which he or she will be especially remembered.

Spirit himself/herself: (**7**) is a closer look at the overall picture of the deceased, particularly examining his or her beliefs, thoughts, and actions.

His/her "house": (**8**), as mentioned, refers to those who were especially close to spirit when alive—the really close friends, whether blood relatives or not.

Hope and fears: (**9**) is self-explanatory, dealing with the hopes and fears that were prevalent in spirit's life.

The final outcome: (**10**) is known insofar as it was death, yet that may not be the *final* outcome, for there are those who are forgotten almost as soon as they die while there are those who are talked about—praised or vilified!—for many years afterward.

Now that we've established the meanings of the positions of the cards, let's look at the cards themselves. How do you read them?

I'd recommend using such a tarot deck as the Rider-Waite, since in that deck all of the cards have full scenes for each card. Some decks show only "the numbers." In other words, the Seven of Swords (for example) simply shows seven swords; the Three of Pentacles shows three pentacles; the Eight of Cups shows eight cups; and so on. But decks such as the Rider-Waite have full scenes that incorporate the seven swords, three pentacles, or eight cups. Some of these scenes are quite elaborate while others are fairly simple, but they all give you more than the basic number of swords, cups, or whatever.

Turn over the card as you come to it, in order; *don't turn over all of them at the start.* As you turn the card face up, you will be struck by one particular item on that card, as your eyes are directed by spirit. One thing above all others will seem important to you, and it won't necessarily have anything to do with the immediate symbology, suit, or value of the card. Let's take the Major Arcana's "Death" card as an example. Books on the tarot will tell you that this card symbolizes transformation and unexpected change. It can also be destruction followed by renewal—death and rebirth. There are also meanings suggested for when the card is found upside down . . . ignore all of these. In using the tarot for spirit communication, what you see is what you get! Look at the card the right way up, no matter how it first comes to you.

On this "Death" card (incidentally, you can ignore these titles on the Major Arcana cards . . . "Death" has nothing to do with an actual, literal death), there is a somewhat complex scene of a skeletal figure in armor astride a white horse. He carries a banner with a large rose on it. Before him stands a priest, with two young figures kneeling beside him. An apparently dead king, his crown beside him, lies almost under the horse's hooves. In the background there are two towers with a sun either rising or setting between them. Closer is a lake with a boat similar to a Viking vessel. There are many other smaller details. When you turn over this card, your eyes will fasten on one particular item. *This is what is significant so far as spirit is concerned*; this is the message or part of the message that spirit is bringing to you.

For example, let's say that your eyes are instantly drawn to the boat on the lake. You immediately (or with a little research!) realize that the spirit you are contacting—let's stick with Uncle Charles for an example—was a great lover of sailing. Perhaps he had a boat and would sail on the local lake, as often as he could get away. As you study the card, you may then recognize other items that are significant, but the boat is the main one. It is spirit saying, "Here is part of my proof of survival. Here is an identifier." Now look at that "identifier" in the context of the position in the layout.

Let's say that it was actually position **9** that produced this Death card. The meaning of **9** is "hopes and fears." You can then relate the boat to Uncle Charles's hopes and fears in order to get an even stronger recognition point. Perhaps Uncle Charles had always loved sailing but at the same time had a fear of falling overboard and drowning! In fact, perhaps Uncle Charles had never actually owned a boat but had only dreamed of owning one because of this fear. This, then—the boat as focal point together with the meaning of the card's position—gives a very strong endorsement of the fact that you are indeed in touch with the spirit of Uncle Charles. The rest of the cards in the complete layout will work the same way, so that, at the end, you will have a complete picture of your departed Uncle Charles.

It is the object of Spiritualists to prove the continuation of life after what is termed death. Working with the tarot can do exactly that, and more. For not only will you get confirmation of spirit, but in the same way—through examining and interpreting the cards—you can receive vital messages from spirit.

And you can receive messages without going to the trouble of doing a full layout. At any time, you can take the cards, shuffle them, and then cut them to look at just one

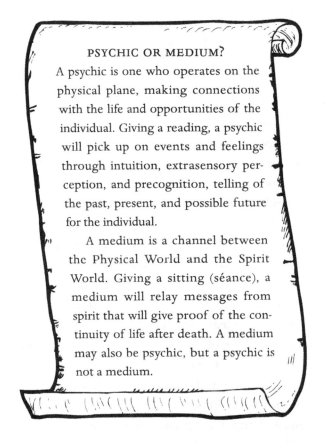

PSYCHIC OR MEDIUM?

A psychic is one who operates on the physical plane, making connections with the life and opportunities of the individual. Giving a reading, a psychic will pick up on events and feelings through intuition, extrasensory perception, and precognition, telling of the past, present, and possible future for the individual.

A medium is a channel between the Physical World and the Spirit World. Giving a sitting (séance), a medium will relay messages from spirit that will give proof of the continuity of life after death. A medium may also be psychic, but a psychic is not a medium.

card. Using that same "what strikes you first" method, you can get a message from spirit. You might even make two or three cuts in order to have what amounts to a conversation with spirit. Sometimes this works to bring you an answer to something you have asked spirit in a meditation.

With any regular séance with a medium, there are frequently facts revealed that are not immediately obvious. Many times you have to check with other relatives, or dig through old photographs and letters, to see that the evidence presented is valid. So it may be with what you get from the tarot cards. In this example, initially you may have no idea what the connection is between Uncle Charles and sailing; it may take quite a bit of research to find that the focus on the sailing boat was an important one. This is why it's important to keep careful records of everything that you get. Write down everything you see in the cards, even—or especially—when it doesn't immediately click. You might have turned over that Death card, in the hopes and fears position, and been drawn to the boat on the surface of the lake, and it might have meant absolutely nothing to you. But by writing it down and then later checking it out, you'll find that it does make a remarkable impression on you when you discover that it *is* a valid and important point in verifying the continued existence of Uncle Charles.

Runes

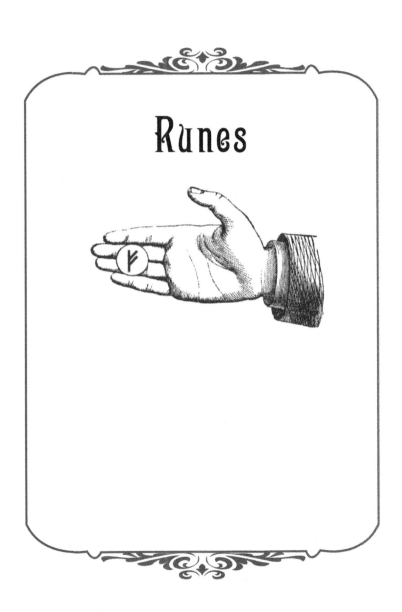

The word *rune* means "secret" or "mystery," coming from the Old Low German word *raunen*, "to cut" or "to carve." This since runes were originally carved into wood and cut into stone. For ease of carving, the runes are made up of all straight lines. Odin, the mythological All-Father and leader of the Norse deities, was the one who discovered the runes. Once, as a sacrifice, he hung from the World Tree *Yggdrasil* for nine days and nights, pierced with a spear. He was then able to lift up the magical runes, which brought secret knowledge to humankind.

Runes were never employed as a utilitarian method of writing, since each letter had a magical meaning. As Ralph Elliott puts it in his book *Runes: An Introduction*, "Communication . . . remained a secondary function of runic writing throughout its long history; much more common was the use of runes to invoke higher powers to affect and influence the lives and fortunes of men."[8]

Those "higher powers," from our point of view, were the spirits.

---

8. Elliott, *Runes: An Introduction*, 2.

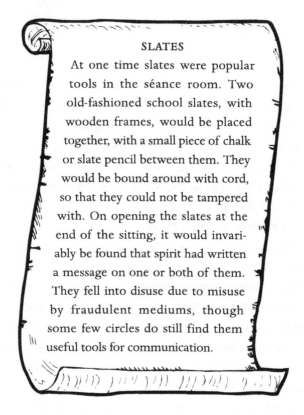

SLATES

At one time slates were popular tools in the séance room. Two old-fashioned school slates, with wooden frames, would be placed together, with a small piece of chalk or slate pencil between them. They would be bound around with cord, so that they could not be tampered with. On opening the slates at the end of the sitting, it would invariably be found that spirit had written a message on one or both of them. They fell into disuse due to misuse by fraudulent mediums, though some few circles do still find them useful tools for communication.

These days, for divination purposes—and for our own spirit communication—individual runes are marked on separate pieces of wood, stone, ceramic, or other material, and used as sets for casting, like the casting of lots in sortilege or the throwing of dice.

It can be fun to make your own runes. One method is to take a length of wood, such as from a broken tree branch, about ¾-inch in diameter, and to cut it into slices (a bandsaw can be useful for this, but a regular hand saw will also work). The slices should be about ¼ inch thick. Make a total of twenty-five of them. On one side of each slice mark one of the rune symbols—three sets of eight, plus a blank. You can use a marking pen or paint, but a more traditional way is to use a wood burner and burn on the symbol, or just carve it in. The individual runes can then be sanded and, if you wish, varnished.

To use the runes for a solitary séance, they should all be placed in a bag and shaken up to mix them thoroughly. Then, either concentrating on the spirit you wish to connect with or keeping the mind blank and open (if there is no one particular spirit you wish to contact), reach in and draw out one rune. Hold it in the palm of your hand and study it. What does the shape of the rune make you think of? For example, the rune Jera, ⫯ , might make you think of two people (seeing them as stick figures), one lifting the other. Or you might be reminded of a trailer hitch connecting up to the towing vehicle.

We may see strange things—or be reminded of strange things—when we study these different shapes. But however strange and offbeat it may seem, write it down. It may be that the one symbol triggers a whole host of thoughts. Write down all of them. This is spirit coming through with information for you.

You can just work with one rune or you can pull a number of them, such as three different ones. (I wouldn't pull too many, perhaps five at the most.) You can then look at them individually and also as connecting units. Look at them upright and look at them sideways. If you draw the blank rune, you may very well still get a thought coming into your head. Write it down. Take your time doing this, but, by the same token, don't strain . . . if nothing comes, then make a note of which rune it was and pass on to another.

When you have got, and recorded, whatever comes, then compare that to the traditional meanings of the runes. You may be surprised at how what "just came into your head" ties in with the traditional meaning of that particular rune, and then, by extension, you may be shocked to discover that it all points to one particular spirit and his or her background.

There were many variations on the runes, found in different geographical areas. The earliest had twenty-four characters and is named Futhark, after the first six letters, and for the sake of simplicity these are the runes we will consider for the solitary séance. They are divided

ᚠ f	ᚢ u	ᚦ th	ᚨ a	ᚱ r	ᚲ k	ᚷ g	ᚹ w
ᚺ h	ᚾ n	ᛁ i	ᛃ j	ᛇ ae	ᛈ p	ᛉ z	ᛊ s
ᛏ t	ᛒ b	ᛖ e	ᛗ m	ᛚ l	ᛜ ng	ᛞ d	ᛟ o

into three groups of eight runes, with each group known as an *ætt*, or *ættir* (meaning "number of eight"). These groups, in turn, are known as Freya's Eight, Hagal's Eight, and Tiw's Eight. A blank rune is usually added to these to bring the total up to twenty-five. What follows are the traditional meanings of the runes.

Freya's Eight

ᚠ FEHU: This is known as the Rune of Possessions, which includes material gains. It deals with fulfillment, financial success, and also perseverance. Its original meaning is believed to have been to do with cattle, or "mobile wealth." It is also "the price to pay" for success and happiness.

ᚢ URUZ: This rune is connected with creation . . . the original creation of the world. It represents force, inner strength, and also wisdom. The name comes from *au-roch*, the European bison. It is good fortune if no risks are taken.

Þ THURISAZ: The Rune of Protection, a defense against invaders. It is the great spirit, a giant. Take no risks with this rune and beware of petty annoyances.

ᚠ ANSUZ: This indicates that something important is to be said. It deals with communication, wisdom, knowledge, mental agility, and creative expression. It also indicates rebirth.

ᚱ RAIDHO: This is the rune of travel, rhythm, movement—a journey. Its name comes from the Danish word for "wheel." It ties in with the wheel of the year, the natural flow of the year's passing.

< KAUNAZ: This is the rune of knowledge, yet it also ties in with cremation and the eternal fire. It can indicate inner enlightenment.

X GEBO: The crossing of two forces. This rune can also symbolize a gift or an exchange of gifts. There can be interaction and also balance.

Þ WUNJO: The rune looks a little like a flag or a weathervane. It symbolizes joy and hope, also pleasure. It ties in very strongly with spirits, the spirits in all things. Kinship and fellowship are in this rune.

Hagal's Eight

H HAGLAZ: This rune shows a connection or merging between two realms of being (the Spirit World and the Physical World), leading to harmony, transformation, and also protection.

ᛝ NAUTHIZ: The word means "need" and can imply an actual need and also represent the need-fire (the fire started by rubbing together two sticks). It can be the potential that releases you from your needs.

I ISA: Originally representing an icicle, this rune is straight, vertical, and unmoving, holding everything together in its present form. It stops all activity; it is static.

ᛃ JERA: The rune of cycles . . . summer/winter, for example. It is completion, natural law, and continuation. The word *jera* means "year." It cannot act against the natural order of things.

ᛇ EIHWAZ: This rune symbolizes the vertical axis of the world tree Yggdrasil, a mighty yew tree. It is one of the most powerful runes. It represents communication, death, regeneration, knowledge. It also touches on magic and dreaming.

ᛈ PERDHO: The rune of luck/chance; a lot that may be cast. Manifestation, chance, wisdom, kinship.

Y ALGIZ: Protective forces. Sanctuary, refuge, power. The power of human spirit moving and evolving.

ϟ SOWULO: The rune of the sun; the solar wheel. It is partnership, as well as journey and transformation plus understanding. It can be used for education, and it counterbalances Isa, thus reactivating that which had become static.

Tiw's Eight

↑ TEIWAZ: The rune of leadership and powerful guidance. It is the point of the spear. Justice, support, loyalty, and self-sacrifice. This is a rune for faith.

ß BERKANA: The nurturing rune that brings to life and protects. It is rebirth and growth, transition and spirit. Berkana is the great Earth Goddess, Mother of All. It is rebirth of spirit, tying in with springtime.

M EHWAZ: The rune of duality, partnership, interaction, and harmony. There is also movement indicated. It shows the energy of the warmer part of the year. This rune is sometimes referred to as the "horse rune."

M MANNAZ: This rune symbolizes the divine aspect within every person. Humankind is the product of divine energy, bringing intelligence and reason. It is the bridge between the worlds. It is the partnership between human and divine.

⊦ LAGUZ: This rune is the energy of life itself, yet it also contains the idea of death and what comes after. "Going with the flow" is incorporated into this rune, suggesting fluidity.

◊ INGUZ: This rune is associated with fertility, gestation, and also castration. It is very much a rune of energy. It ties in with initiation and with rebirth on all its levels.

ᛞ DAGAZ: The balance between day and night. The name means "day," and the emphasis is therefore on awakening, light, sunrise, and dawn. Yet also it deals with sunset and twilight. In that sense it is a liminal rune.

ᛟ OTHILA: This is the rune of heredity and property. It is the sacred land and the bond between that and people. It is ancestral heritage and tribal property. It is generally viewed as a rune of prosperity.

Dominoes
and Numerology

ominoes seem to date from twelfth-century China, where they were used for divination long before they were adopted for game playing. It was not until the eighteenth century that the sets of tiles were found in England, Italy, and France. An old Romani (Gypsy) belief is that the dominoes should not be consulted more than once in a moon's span. For the purposes of the solitary séance, however, I think this can be disregarded.

A general overview of the dominoes indicates that the sixes are connected with good luck, fives with jobs and careers, fours with matters of finance, threes with family and close friends, twos with love, and ones with journeys and travel in general.

Start with all the dominoes laid out, *face down*, and move them around to thoroughly mix them. If you have a particular deceased person you would like to connect with, then concentrate on that person as you mix the tiles. There are a number of different "drawings" you can do. The simplest is to turn over just one of the tiles, but we'll look at different ways that spirit might communicate. There are traditional meanings for all the tiles, but in addition to reading these, see if you get any sense of what spirit is trying to say just from the "feel" of the domino. Sometimes it is sufficient just to make the connection with spirit—who is present and also handling the tiles—and thereby attune to what is being communicated. There is a relationship to psychometry in this. (The next chapter in this book explains psychometry.)

You can, if you wish, turn over a number of dominoes together. As with runes, I'd recommend not doing more than three or so at one time, however. Read what the meaning is and see if you can connect that to what you know of the deceased; in this way, you will get your confirmation of the spirit connection and the validation of the "life after death." Don't forget to make notes.

Note: The "traditional meanings" (for the domino reading of a living person seeking to look into his or her present and future) I give in italics.[9] I then give one interpretation of that as it might be applied to the solitary séance. Do your own interpretations also, for it is *your* connection to spirit that will give the most correct reading.

Double Six: *The marriage of the querent. If already married, then there will be good fortune coming as a result of that marriage.* Indicating that spirit was married, and hap-

---

9. These interpretations are as I gave them in my 2004 book *The Fortune-Telling Book: The Encyclopedia of Divination and Soothsaying*. They are reprinted here with permission from Visible Ink Press.

pily so. If not spirit himself/herself, then spirit came from such a happy union.

Double Five: *A job promotion, to a better paid, higher position.* Spirit had a good job, a good position in his/her employment. It's even possible that spirit was heading for a promotion at the time of passing.

Double Four: *Unexpected money coming in a dramatic way.* Spirit enjoyed an unexpected inheritance, lottery win, or something similar. Another way of interpreting this is that the survivor(s) inherited money as a result of spirit's passing.

Double Three: *The querent will unexpectedly fall in love.* Relating to spirit's love life, either in later years or earlier.

Double Two: *There will be new friends who will become close and dear.* As a result of spirit's passing, you—or other survivor(s)—gain new friends and acquaintances.

Double One: *A wonderful, and very enjoyable, vacation journey is on its way.* This could refer to spirit's feelings about passing! It could be that he or she had worked extremely hard up until the time of death, and so now, being in spirit is much like a "vacation."

Double Blank: *Extreme caution needs to be exercised.* This could indicate many things. For example, there might be some form of litigation tied in to the passing of this spirit. The survivors need to tread carefully and be on their guard for a while.

This gives you an idea of how the traditional meanings may be applied to spirit. With the balance I'll leave you to do your own interpretations (since they are usually very personal), which you can base on the following traditional readings:

Six/Five: If you're looking for a job, persevering will bring you to a good one. Similarly, if you are looking for love, don't be discouraged by rebuffs; success awaits you. This tile indicates luck in purchasing real estate but the possibility of being cheated buying jewelry, silverware, or a watch. If you are waiting on a possible inheritance, there's a good chance you will get it.

Six/Four: Early marriage followed by much happiness. Children will be equally divided between boys and girls. When grown, they will all leave home early— the girls to get married and the boys to jobs. Neither wealth nor poverty is indicated with this tile.

Six/Three: A domino for constancy and affection. It shows an early marriage with much happiness and no troubles to mar it. There will also be honors and riches. There is a slight possibility of death in middle age, but if you survive that, you will live to a ripe old age.

Six/Two: Excellent domino for lovers, foretelling a happy marriage. Those looking for luck in business will find more profits than they expected. However, if there are any dishonest schemes, they will be "rewarded" with disaster.

Six/One: To young married people, this tile indicates that they will be better off in later life than they are now. It can also indicate that there will be a second marriage that will be better than the first.

Six/Blank: This tile is an indicator of death to someone near to you, be it a close friend or an acquaintance. It may also indicate the death of an animal.

Five/Four: This is not a good tile where money is concerned. If you have money, you may lose it or you may find that you owe more than you realized.

Five/Three: You will never be poor, but you may never be rich. You will always have sufficient. If you already have money, you will not gain much more. It indicates much the same where love and sex is concerned—status quo.

Five/Two: This is a reasonably fair card for women but not so for men. If in love, or married, the woman may turn out to have a short temper. A marriage may turn out to appear happy and successful on the outside but will deteriorate and be unhappy in the end. Financial speculation, for a man, will not be successful.

Five/One: For those fond of excitement, this is a good tile. There is the possibility of an invitation to an event that will thrill you. If money is expected, there will be disappointment. A young woman may find an admirer who is rich but rough. She will discard him and marry another.

Five/Blank: To a man, this tile implies that there is a certain amount of dishonesty present, with a tendency to gambling or sex. To a woman, this indicates an unhappy love affair.

Four/Three: Those who turn this tile will marry young, live happily, and will not have more than one child. There is neither poverty nor riches here. Married persons who have children already will face the possibility of a long separation and even a second marriage.

Four/Two: There will be a change in your circumstances, which could be for the better or for the worse. It may be something slight or something that will be very traumatic. If you have offended anyone dear to you, this tile shows that you will soon make up with them.

Four/One: Referring to married couples, the more children in the marriage, the more the financial position will deteriorate. Those who are unmarried may soon get married, with the same results. If there are no children, the bank account will grow.

Four/Blank: This is an unfortunate tile for lovers. It foretells arguments and quarrels, possibly separations. If you should trust a friend with a secret, the secret will not be kept. There is also an indication, with this tile, that your partner is a believer in the occult.

Three/Two: This is a good tile for the following: lovemaking, marriage, recovery of stolen property, travel, speculation, collecting on a debt, planting a crop. It is, however, a bad tile for gamblers.

Three/One: A young woman turning this tile will be likely to lose her virginity. A married woman will be approached by a man with a view to having an affair. For a man, this foretells the loss of money through illicit sex. It is not a favorable domino for anyone.

Three/Blank: Your sweetheart is artful and deceitful. If you are married, the wife will be shrewish and vain; the husband will be dull, slow, and not very bright. This tile may also indicate that you will be invited to a party where you will be attracted to someone, but it will end with a violent quarrel.

Two/One: A woman will marry young and her husband will die young, leaving her wealth and property. She will later remarry. A man will have a life of luxury, will never marry, but will be a favorite of the ladies. Not a good tile for businesspeople, since it foretells losses by failures.

Two/Blank: Poverty and bad luck. This is a tile of good luck for thieves and dishonest people, indicating success in shady dealings. In reference to any possible journey, it indicates a safe passage.

One/Blank: You will have an encounter with a stranger who will bring much unhappiness. If the stranger is female the unhappiness will be long lasting.

❧

Another way to look at dominoes is through numerology. Take the two numbers on the tile, look at them as individual numbers, and then add them together to get a third number. For example, a 6-4 tile will give you the numbers 6, 4, and 10—reduced to 6, 4, and 1. (Two digit numbers, in numerology, are always reduced to single digits, so 10 becomes 1+0=1; 11 becomes 1+1=2; 13 becomes 1+3=4, and so on). With some tiles, of course, where you have a double, you will only have a total of two numbers.

Very simple numerology would give the following attributes of spirit:

1: A leader and driving force. An explorer. Tends to be impatient.

2: Sensitive, emotional person. Domestic and fond of the home.

3: Interested in the material rather than the spiritual. A scientist or investigator.

4: Strong intuitive tendencies. Interested in occult/metaphysics. Things out of the ordinary.

5: Physically and mentally active. Inquiring. Fond of reading and research. Friendly.

6: Good looking, gentle, and refined. Very sociable. Excellent diplomat.

7: Psychic. Introvert who thinks a lot. Mysterious. Interested in chemistry and psychology.

8: Little sense of humor. Cold and pessimistic. Enjoys hard work. Good at finances.

9: Emotional and can be jealous. Loyal and close to family. Can be impulsive.

Psychometry

Psychometry is the ability to hold an object and, from its vibrations, to "pick up" details of those people who have been in contact with it. A medium can take a ring, watch, necklace, or similar object that had belonged to the deceased (even a letter written by the deceased can be used) and, from holding the object, can tell a great deal about the person. Not only can details of the person be gathered, but also information about other people and things that have been in close contract with the object.

The word *psychometry* means "soul measure," from the Greek *psyche* and *metron*. Theoretically, everything that has ever existed has left its mark on the ether. On a broad scale, this can be seen with people and events leaving indelible marks in the ether that become ghosts and hauntings. Such remnants can be picked up by psychics in the same way that, on a smaller scale, psychics and mediums can pick up emanations through psychometry.

Most people have the ability to psychometrize. The "ordinary" person can hold an old pocket watch in their hands and, after a few moments concentration, can give a fair description of the person who had owned the watch. A common object such as a coin seldom works, since it has been passed through so many different hands and has not, therefore, absorbed from just one individual.

In Spiritualism there is an expression: "Spirit speaks first." In other words, the very first impressions you get are probably the ones coming directly from spirit. The longer you wait and think about an object, the more likely it is that your logical mind will come into play and try to "explain" the object rather than going strictly by its vibrations.

An object that belonged to a deceased loved one, then, can be a very effective tool for making contact. It can work on two levels: it can give the physical contact that unveils the hidden emanations, and it can also help bridge the gap across the two worlds, allowing spirit to more easily come through.

You can start your psychometrizing as soon as you start your meditation, holding the object while you meditate. This will often induce spirit to come into your meditation and speak to you directly. It can also be an aid, in that you can hold the object in one hand while doing automatic writing with the other hand. As with all such experiments, write down what you get. Much of it will seem complete nonsense, but write it down anyway. It's only in the later verification process that you can see just how accurate you can be.

Different mediums have different ways to hold the object. Many will simply hold it lightly in one or both hands. Others will hold it to their forehead or over the area of the heart. Some will even hold it over the abdomen or on the top of their head. It would seem, then, that one of the chakra points is recognized as a suitable contact point.

In the same way, you can get different types of impressions. You might become conscious of a taste. Perhaps your deceased Aunt Cora used to drink inordinate amounts of coffee and, as you hold her old wedding band, you find that you get the taste of coffee in your mouth (known as *clairgustance* or *clairhambience*). Or perhaps it's Uncle Howard's cheap cigars that you suddenly smell (known as *clairalience*), or you swear you can hear the sound of Grandpa's old upright piano (*clairaudience*). All of these things, of course, are valid in proving the continuation of life after that change we term death. This is especially so if we have to check with relatives and/or friends before we discover that Cora drank lots of coffee or that Grandpa secretly played great ragtime in his basement.

Gather personal items that once belonged to your loved one and see what you can glean from them. You may get absolutely nothing one day and a whole wealth of material another day. As mentioned, keep records of what you do, what you held, how you held it, and what results you got.

Bibliomancy

A very old method of divination is *bibliomancy*, which is simply opening a book at random and reading the first sentence your eyes fall upon. This works well for spirit communication, since it is spirit that is directing the opening of the book and the sentence seen. In times past, the Christian Bible was the book preferred by many for the practice of bibliomancy, but for our purposes the wider range we can give spirit, the better the results are likely to be.

I would suggest facing a shelf of books or, better yet, a whole case of books. If your eyes are right away drawn to one book in particular, take out that book and set it on the table in front of you. But if there is no immediate "grabber," then close your eyes, concentrate on the spirit you wish to communicate with, and gently run your fingers along the back of the books. Stop when you feel you are at the right one—spirit will let you know. Take out that book and lay it on the table in front of you.

Now close your eyes and do a short meditation, concentrating on the spirit you wish to contact or just opening your mind to any of a number of spirits with whom you would feel comfortable. Some people say a short prayer at this time, though it's not necessary.

It's a good idea to have an opening question in your mind when you start. This gives spirit a "jumping off point," as it were. So think of your question, open your eyes, and open the book at any page. Try to open it cleanly. In other words, don't keep turning pages. Just open it wide at any one page. Without looking down, point to a position on the page with your finger. Now you can look down and read. The sentence that you are indicating should relate in some way to the question you have asked. Whether it does or not (or doesn't seem to), make a note of it. You can then close the book, concentrate on another question, and open the book again at another page indicating another sentence. Do this about five or six times—noting the sentences—before becoming too critical if the sentences don't seem too relevant. Occasionally, it is not the complete sentence that is relevant but just a main word in that sentence.

Re-read through your list of questions and then read through all the sentences/words you got. You should see that spirit is indeed responding to you. It may be that there are not specific answers to the questions themselves, but there are the indicators of contact with the deceased loved one—the proofs of survival.

You don't *have* to ask questions. In fact, it can be a good introduction to simply open the book and indicate the sentences, three or four times, making a note of them. This way there is not the feeling that the sentences have to directly answer what you have asked, but can be a more open contact from spirit, giving the necessary proof of survival.

An alternative to simply opening the book—especially if it is a thick volume—is to riffle through the pages until you sense spirit telling you to stop. You then fully open the book at that page and proceed to point to a word.

Tasseography

Tasseography is the fancy name for tea-leaf reading. It is well suited to the solitary séance, since everything depends upon your interpretation of the pattern of symbols made in the cup by the tea leaves.

There is a small ritual in obtaining the pattern of tea leaves. First of all, the kind of tea used is important. Most suitable is Chinese tea, but any large-leafed variety will work. Ceylon tea or even mint tea has been used very successfully. The cup used is also important. It should be a round one that inside is plain-colored or white. There should be no grooves or ridges that might interfere with the even distribution of the leaves. The cup should also have a handle.

When the tea has been poured (no strainer and no tea bag, of course!), sit with the cup in your hands and—with eyes open or closed—think of the spirit you wish to contact. Then, when you feel ready, sip some of the tea. You should take at least three sips, leaving a small amount in the bottom of the cup. With your right hand, swirl the remaining tea and leaves around in the cup, rotating the cup at least three times. Then up-turn the cup onto the saucer.

Any balance of tea will run out into the saucer, and you can then pick up the cup and look inside.

To interpret, the handle of the cup represents spirit. The closer the symbols are to the handle, the stronger they relate to spirit. In other words, any symbols you see (I'll talk about them in a moment) that are on the inside of the cup *opposite* the position of the handle will have the least connection to spirit, while those next to the handle are very closely associated.

Similarly, as you descend into the base of the cup, so the time prior to spirit's passing increases. That is, what you see represented by a symbol in the very bottom of the cup is connected to what happened to spirit quite some time before his or her passing. A symbol up near the rim of the cup relates to what happened to spirit close to the transition. The depth from the rim of the cup down to the bottom is, then, a time scale.

The symbols made by the groupings of tea leaves will not necessarily look *exactly* like the things they represent. Imagination must be used. It will be found that there is the *suggestion* of, say, a bird or a rabbit, or whatever. These suggestions should be enough to trigger the mind into seeing them fully and seeing all that they represent. Sometimes it happens that the symbols are very distinct, but it won't necessarily be so. What is actually seen is used as a focal point, as a "trigger," for your inherent mediumistic power. Seeing the symbols, and interpreting them, is best done when that interpretation comes from within, rather than from memorizing a list of shapes and symbols and their probable meanings. However, to start with, what follows are some of the traditional meanings and interpretations, as given in a wide variety of books over the years.

Symbols and Their Meanings

Aces: Powerful forces were at work around spirit. The ace of hearts is associated with domestic and social affairs; diamonds with financial affairs; clubs with business, contracts, and lawsuits; spades with sorrow and with delays.

Acorn: Indicates riches if it appears near the handle. On the far side it indicates a business partnership, or the potential for financial assistance through a second party.

Airplane: A biplane shows there was a successful partnership. Any airplane shows swift and successful progression.

Alligator: Great care was needed to avoid injury from those trying to harm spirit.

Alps: Spirit had great aspirations. Nearby symbols may give some idea of time and indicate degree of success.

Anchor: A delay; a holding back. Establishing of roots.

Angel: An indicator of good news.

Ant: Success through spirit's own industry, perseverance, and thrift.

Anvil: Difficulties were followed by financial gains, after much work.

Arc: A segment of a circle shows possible premature retirement or even an accident. An unfinished project.

Arrow: Bad news. It is connected with finance if there are dots around the arrow. Note direction of arrow for indication of which direction the news will come from.

Asterisk: Something concerning spirit needs immediate attention. Clues may be found in nearby symbols.

Axe: There were danger and difficulties in spirit's later life, with the possibility of separation or loss of friends. Spirit had a choice in the matter if it's a double-headed axe.

Baby: There was a new enterprise that might have started new troubles.

Bag: Problems for spirit brought on by unknown enemies, plans, plots, and schemes. The fuller the bag, the bigger the problems.

Bagpipes: There were difficulties in business. High tension brought on ill health.

Ball: Spirit had no control over a variety of ups and downs that took place.

Balloon: A welcome, and needed, rise in fortunes.

Barrel: Spirit had to serve rather than rule. Spirit had vain ambitions and empty dreams.

Basket: A gift or a legacy. If located close to the symbol of a house, then there was an addition to the family.

Bat: Spirit suffered false friends and there was a need to exercise caution.

Bear: Brute force was needed for spirit to overcome obstacles. Stupidity could have led to danger.

Bed: Good fortune unless the bed appears untidy, when it indicates a poor state of mind resulting in poor results.

Bee: Industry on the part of spirit brought prosperity. There was a general change of fortune for the better, with wealth obtained through trade.

Bench: Status quo. Stability.

Bird: There was good news for spirit. (Nearby symbols might elaborate on this.)

Boat: Spirit possibly took a journey and/or had visitors from some distance away.

Book: An open book signifies some sort of revelation that was to spirit's benefit, while a closed book shows there was need for research by spirit.

Boomerang: Spirit's actions came back on him/her, for good or ill.

Boot: If the image is well-formed, it signifies protection from danger. Ill-formed suggests disgrace with loss of position.

Bottle: Something to do with spirit's health. Examine other close symbols.

Bow: A good sign showing that there was the ability to grow.

Bracelet: Possibly a partnership, even a marriage.

Branch: Sign of a birth. A branch with leaves indicates there was a new venture; without leaves there was disappointment.

Bride: Possible troubles and sorrow.

Bridge: A possible way out of difficulties.

Broken lines: Uncertainty. Broken promises.

Broom: Spirit had the chance to clear up a problem.

Buffalo: Risks were taken despite possible danger.

Bull: Profit.

Butterfly: Caution was needed due to frivolous action.

Cabbage: Jealousy.

Cage: Domesticity.

Cake: A celebration.

Camel: Advancement.

Candle: Spirit was a philanthropist of some sort.

Canoe: Spirit visited someone some distance away or was visited by someone from afar.

Carriage: Receipt of benefits.

Cart: Light burdens with profitable trade.

Castle: Spirit advanced to a high position and/or was well regarded by someone with influence.

Cat: There was the possibility of cheating in business. A resting cat means domestic comfort.

Chair: Spirit was trusted and successful. Could also mean a new occupation.

Chicken: Competence, possibly with nervous energy.

Child: Spirit had a natural aptitude that brought success. A number of fresh enterprises added to prosperity.

Chimney: Distinction through service.

Church: Formal occasions; pomp and ceremony. Rituals.

Cigar: Spirit had optimistic dreams.

Cigarette: A frivolous nature.

Circle: Work was completed to near perfection.

Clock: There was a recovery from sickness.

Clover: Spirit was lucky; had extraordinary luck if clover is four-leafed.

Coffin: There was a serious illness. The ending of a plan or phase.

Column: Spirit was admired. Received honors.

Comet: Unexpected news.

Cornucopia: Symbol of plenty and freedom from want.

Cow: Spirit may have been asked for a donation. Had a peaceful and happy existence.

Cradle: New enterprises. A broken cradle indicates there had been trouble.

Cross: Ideas and inspiration.

Crown: Promotion after difficulties.

Cup: Promotion after a sacrifice had been made.

Daffodil: Fulfillment of plans, leading to happiness.

Dagger: A warning was received indicating the need for care.

Deer: A quick decision had been called for. Good news from a distance.

Devil: Possible danger from false friends.

Dice: Gambling losses.

Dog: A sleeping dog indicates peace and quiet. A leaping dog shows cause for celebration. Dogs indicate friendship.

Door: Open to opportunity.

Dot: Emphasizes the meaning and importance of symbols close by.

Dragon: Challenges led to opportunities.

Drum: There was some negative publicity and possibly disturbances or domestic disputes.

Duck: Welcome news.

Dumbbell: Rivalry, with frustrating hard work.

Dwarf: Disappointment and failure.

Eagle: Great success.

Ear: There may have been a scandal.

Egg or oval: The strong possibility of success with new projects.

Eight: Number of Uranus. A sign of genius, invention, and inspiration.

Elephant: Delay leading eventually to success. Strength; wisdom.

Explosion: Violent upsets and disturbances.

Eyeglasses: Care had to be taken in all business dealings.

Face/head: Looking toward the handle is good; away from it is bad. A full face could signify that there were new discoveries.

Fan: An indicator of indiscretions and false friends. Possibly might mean a mild flirtation took place.

Feather: Things were not taken seriously.

Fence: Circumstances were limited.

Fire: Hasty action was called for, following unexpected news.

Fish: Increase, affluence, and opportunities.

Fist: There was a need to guard against impulses.

Five: Number of Jupiter. Good fortune; increase.

Flag: There was a danger sign connected to duty. A chance of special honors.

Flower: A single flower shows that a favor was granted. A bunch of flowers indicates there were many benefits.

Fly: Domestic annoyances. Possible scandal.

Foot: Signifies understanding. Two feet: spirit could move wherever desired.

Fork: Lack of control led to a dilemma.

Fountain: Happiness grew from great success.

Four: Number of Mercury. Reality; completion.

Fox: There may have been a betrayal of trust.

Frog: Misinterpretations.

Fruit: A positive sign of advancement.

Gallows: There was a high chance of financial or social failure.

Garland: See *Flower*.

Gate: An open gate signifies opportunities. A closed one, a barrier.

Ghost: Caution needed; unexpected sources posed danger.

Girl: Signifying great happiness.

Glass: Fragility and honesty.

Goat: Obstinacy as a cause of misfortune.

Grapes: Prosperity, but accompanied by burdens.

Grasshopper: News from a distance.

Grave: News of a death.

Guitar: Happiness brought about through love.

Gun, pistol, revolver, rifle: Need for extra caution. The possibility of hurt from a distance. A rival for love was indicated if it is close to a heart symbol.

Hammer: There was need for persistence due to stress.

Hand: Friendship indicated if the sign is toward the cup handle. If away from handle, then loss of opportunity.

Handcuffs: Frustrations; restraint.

Harp: Harmony. Happiness regarding a romantic situation.

Hat: Ambition, fresh ideas, possibly a new occupation.

Heart: Great happiness. Close friendship and/or union.

Hill: Accomplishment. The higher the hill, the better were the results.

Hive: Signifying home. Great success indicated if bees swarm about the hive.

Horn: Good news.

Horse/pony: Close friendships. A galloping horse means good news from someone dear. The arrival of a lover is indicated by just a horse's head.

Hourglass: Time was running out, calling for swift action.

House: Safety; possessions. A contented life.

Insect: Troubles and vexations along with small irritations.

Ivy: Loyal friends.

Jug: Influential friendships. Spirit helped others and, in so doing, helped himself/herself.

Kangaroo: Unexpected travel plans.

Kettle: Domestic happiness.

Key: There were important decisions to be made leading to possible new paths ahead. There was a need to give due consideration to new proposals.

Kite: Unusual ambitions that might have led to reaching new heights.

Ladder: Opportunities. If dots are near, connected to finances.

Lamb/sheep: New ideas leading to changes.

Lamp: Recovery of lost property. Previously hidden items revealed.

Leaf: News, letters, messages. Many leaves means good news.

Leg: Strength; fortitude. Note the direction in which the leg faces.

Letter: News was coming. Look for other symbols nearby to determine whether good or bad.

Lighthouse: There was trouble ahead with caution needed.

Lines: Whether straight or curved, indicate directions to be taken; roads, rivers, railroads.

Lion: Supremacy. Recognition of spirit's leadership.

Loaf of Bread: Plenty; lack or worry about the immediate future.

Lock: A difficult problem that needed to be solved.

Man: A visitor of significance. If the figure is facing the handle, then the visitor stayed for a while. If facing away, it was a brief visit.

Medal: Spirit's work received some special recognition.

Mermaid: There was temptation that needed strength to overcome.

Monk: There was some deception.

Monkey: Flattery led to the possibility of danger.

Moon: There were new ideas and undertakings, possibly with a romantic link.

Mountains: Spirit was faced with challenges and attained heights only with great effort.

Mouse: Opportunities were overlooked. There may have been a theft. Possible poverty for a period.

Mushroom: Expansion and growth.

Nail: Malice was directed against spirit, though only feelings got hurt.

Necklace: Symbolizes many admirers.

Nine: The number of Neptune. Spiritual perception.

Numbers are important and can refer to hours, days, weeks, etc. They should be applied to other symbols close by. They might also be tied in to numerology. (See the "Dominoes and Numerology" chapter.)

One: Number of the Sun. Happiness, success, dignity, honors.

Owl: There was failure of a new enterprise.

Ox: Someone in a high position became a friend of spirit, helping toward prosperity.

Pagoda: For a time spirit moved in distinguished company.

Palm Tree: Spirit was in a position to retire at any time.

Parachute: An opportunity to escape from danger.

Peacock: Luxury and elegance.

Pig: Good luck. Although never wanting for food, there was always the danger of overindulgence.

Pipe: There was a respite, giving spirit time to re-plan.

Pumpkin: Diplomacy.

Puppy: Indecision.

Pyramid: A secret was revealed, helping spirit to advance.

Quiver: A message was sent to spirit.

Question mark: The unknown. Frustration.

Rabbit: Timidity. Spirit needed to be more assertive.

Racquet (tennis): There was a competition. If the handle of the racquet is toward the cup's handle, spirit triumphed. If away from it, spirit lost.

Rainbow: Spirit experienced hope and encouragement.

Rake: Indicates a careful and industrious nature.

Raven, rook, or crow: Spirit had a roving nature; tended to hoard things.

Ring: Possible partnership: look for initials anywhere near this symbol.

Rose: Possible marriage.

Saddle: A journey.

Saw: Hard work.

Scaffold: Possibility of legal action against spirit.

Scales: There was some sort of judgement made involving spirit. If the scales shown are tipping toward the cup handle, then it ended favorably.

Scissors: Confusion and misunderstandings.

Scorpion: Dangerous business dealings.

Seven: The number of Saturn. Wisdom, balance, perfection.

Shark: Spirit encountered someone of a predatory disposition.

Ship: Spirit's efforts led to success and good fortune.

Shoe: There was a message of good news.

Six: Number of Venus. Cooperation, harmony, love, peace, satisfaction.

Skeleton: There were lean times and possibly sickness.

Skull: Care was needed in dealing with others.

Sleigh: There was rapid progress with little opposition.

Snake: Healing and wisdom. Business caution was needed.

Spade: Indicates steady employment with appropriate compensation.

Spear: Physical injury or injury to spirit's reputation.

Spider: Possible entrapment.

Spiral: Spirit slowly but surely made progress.

Spoon: Spirit was not afraid to energetically "stir things up" if necessary.

Square: Acknowledgement of limitations.

Star: Opportunities that could lead to good fortune.

Steeple: Spirit possessed ambitions; high aspirations.

Stocks/pillory: Frustration. Feelings of being held back.

Submarine: Spirit had hidden enemies.

Sun: Success, bringing great happiness.

Swan: Spirit was lucky in love.

Sword: Depending on which way it is pointing, there could have been a challenge (toward the cup handle) or a protection (away from handle).

Table: There was a reunion.

Teapot: Spirit had many meetings and consultations.

Tent: Spirit found temporary shelter from approaching troubles.

Three: Number of Mars. Possible accident, fire, or a quarrel.

Torch: Spirit possessed a pioneering spirit.

Tortoise/turtle: Spirit made slow but steady advancement after a great deal of hard work.

Train: There was travel, bringing change.

Tree: A wish was fulfilled.

Triangle: Always a sign of good luck and success.

Trident: Possible promotion to a position of respect.

Two: Number of the Moon. Dualism. Relationship of opposites.

Umbrella: If open, it was protection. If closed, it was frustration.

Vase: Service to others.

Violin: Spirit was a very private and independent person, an individualist.

Volcano: A passionate person, possibly with an explosive temper.

Vulture: Theft might have been involved.

Web: Spirit should have trod carefully and listened to advice. May have got caught up in a difficult situation.

Whale: There was a big project that would not bring spirit returns for some years.

Wheel: Spirit needed to exercise patience in order to make progress.

Wig: Deception.

Windmill: Big rewards came from plans that initially seemed too pretentious.

Wings: Mobility.

Wishbone: There was an inheritance.

Witch: Wisdom and good advice was available to spirit.

Wolf: Spirit showed great cleverness.

Woman: Spirit received news from a visiting woman.

Yacht: Spirit was aware that news was coming before learning what it was.

Yoke: There was a time of having to take orders from someone else.

Zebra: Special distinction and recognition by spirit.

Flame Messages

Flame messages (technically known as *pyroscopy*) are a form of spirit communication popular at several Spiritualist communities. This is a variation on *lampadomancy*, which consists of divining by the form, color, and various movements of the light from a candle or lamp. Flame reading, as used in spirit communication, deals more with interpreting the smudge left on a sheet of paper by the burning wick of a candle than it does on the actual burning of the flame itself.

Before using any candle, many people like to "dress" or "bless" the item. This is done using pure olive oil. The dressing is done from the center of the candle outward to the ends. Hold the candle at one end and rub it with oil from the center out toward the far end, using just enough oil to very lightly coat the candle. Then take hold of that other end and rub from the center out toward the other end, so that the entire candle has been rubbed with the olive oil. See the illustration on the next page.

At the time you are doing this "dressing," concentrate your thoughts on the person in spirit with whom you wish to connect.

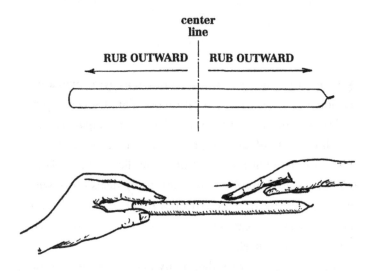

When the candle is ready, sit and meditate for a few more moments on that person and then light the candle. Take a sheet of paper—any size will do, though a regular 8½" x 11" is good—and hold it against your body, over your heart. Hold the paper by the top and bottom edges. If you have any particular question you want to ask, then concentrate on that question.

Now take the paper and hold it over the candle flame with the side that was against your body downward in contact with the flame. Move the paper around, back and forth, and in circles . . . you'll need to keep it moving so that it doesn't catch fire. You should also hold it down

close enough to the flame that a black, or grey, mark is left on the paper. Do this for a few moments and then remove the paper, turning it over so that you can see the image, and examine it.

What you will see, at first glance, may seem to be just a jumble of sooty lines that are quite arbitrary. But the more you study them, the more you will discover. There will be actual faces and figures in the swirls; letters and numbers may be there. Give your imagination full range. Turn the paper around and view it from all directions. Make a note of everything you see, no matter how irrelevant it may seem. Many times what comes through—as in so much of spirit communication—is symbolic. A knowledge of, or reference to, a book on dream symbology can be a great help (see also pages 48–70 in this book). What you see and can make out will be connected in some way with spirit, perhaps tying in with spirit's early life, profession, hobbies, friends, or the like. It will be typical of the evidential material found in other forms of spirit communication.

Fire Spirits

Pyromancy involves divining by the flames caused by a burned sacrifice. We don't need to sacrifice anything or anyone in order to communicate with spirits! Communicating with spirit through the burning of a fire is closer to what is known as *anthracomancy*, named after the anthracite coal that was best for that purpose. Anthracite is a hard, glossy-surfaced coal that burns with very little smoke. As the coal burns, it goes through a stage during which it is a red and yellow mass of hot ashes, retaining the original shape of the piled coals for a while before finally crumbling to nothing. These red-hot ashes are where it is possible to see and imagine all sorts of shapes, faces, figures, and the like, restricted only by the imagination.

As a child growing up in England, where coal fires were the norm, I spent many long winter's nights listening to the radio (in the days before television!) and gazing into these red-hot embers. I saw castles and dragons, as well as people and all sorts of other figures.

Making such a fire (to a lesser extent, a wood fire can produce the same effects) and gazing into it after meditating on, and calling upon, deceased loved ones is a wonderful way to make contact and to present the means for that spirit to get back to you. The faces, figures, and places seen in such a fire-gazing can be particularly relevant to the deceased, providing the very evidence needed to confirm the identity and background of the spirit.

One of the joys of this sort of communication is that, over a few minutes, the scenes and faces built up in the ashes can change as those ashes collapse and produce new images. It is almost possible to have a "conversation" with spirit in this way.

The embers, as they burn down, can be given a brief new life by sprinkling them with a handful of salt or sugar.

Spirit Photography

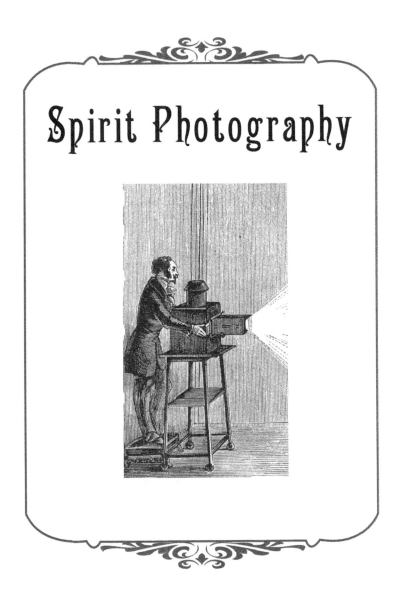

Spirit photography gained an unsavory reputation in the early days of photography because there were so many frauds producing "spirit photographs" by using double exposure. Yet that doesn't mean that *all* spirit photographs were fraudulent. Far from it. There were many produced that seemingly had no logical explanation.

When William H. Mumler, one of the pioneers of spirit photography, was approached by a man and asked to photograph a lady—her name was given as Mrs. Tyndall—who had recently lost her husband, Mumler agreed to do so. The lady later arrived, heavily veiled and dressed in typical Victorian mourning. Mumler posed her in a chair and had her briefly remove her veil for the actual photographing. Later, when the plates were developed, the resultant picture showed her sitting in the chair but with the image of a man standing behind her. Mumler commented that it looked like the late President Lincoln. The supposed Mrs. Tyndall said, "Yes, it probably is. I am his widow—Mary Todd Lincoln."

At a solitary séance, it is not even necessary to have a camera. From a photographic supply store, purchase some photographic paper . . . the sort used for printing

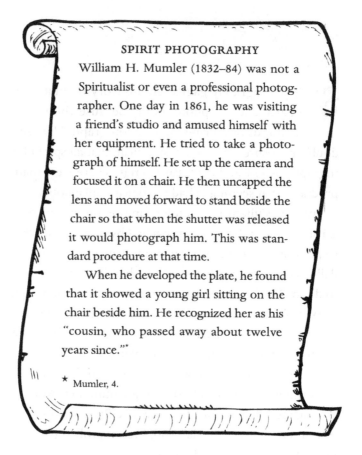

SPIRIT PHOTOGRAPHY

William H. Mumler (1832–84) was not a Spiritualist or even a professional photographer. One day in 1861, he was visiting a friend's studio and amused himself with her equipment. He tried to take a photograph of himself. He set up the camera and focused it on a chair. He then uncapped the lens and moved forward to stand beside the chair so that when the shutter was released it would photograph him. This was standard procedure at that time.

When he developed the plate, he found that it showed a young girl sitting on the chair beside him. He recognized her as his "cousin, who passed away about twelve years since."*

★ Mumler, 4.

photographs. This is light-sensitive and is kept in a light-tight envelope. Take it into a dark room (this could be a closet, preferably at night when there is no extraneous light to seep in) along with a pair of scissors and a roll of aluminum foil. Take out one sheet of the paper. In the dark, take the scissors and cut the sheet into about eight, ten, or a dozen sections. Wrap each piece in aluminum foil, so that when you take it back into the light it will still be light-proof. Then take them with you when you want to do your solitary-séance spirit photography.

Sit as at the other forms of séance described in this book. Start with a meditation, building the white light, and then proceed to a gentle singing of something melodic and light. Or you may prefer to simply hum. Now, take one of the aluminum-enclosed pieces of paper and sit with it held between the palms of your hands. You can also try this with it held over your heart, over the third eye, over the solar plexus—in other words, wherever you feel or find that the psychic energy flows best, wherever you find that you get the best results.

Concentrate your thoughts on the spirit you want to contact. If you have a photograph of the spirit or some item that belonged to him or her, then have it there with you, where you can see it and concentrate on it. Ask—mentally or vocally—for spirit to come and join you, to place his or her image on the photographic paper. You can even say something like "I'd like to take your photograph! Please show yourself to me."

Keep up this concentration for as long as you are able. You can give yourself a short break, if necessary, and then continue with a second piece of the sealed paper. Try as many as you feel comfortable doing. After your séance, you will then need to develop these papers. It's easy enough to do, with the right chemicals again obtained from a photographic supply store. Or you can take them to a photographer and have him or her develop them for you.

On the pieces of paper you may well see an image that relates to, or is even a complete portrait of, the spirit you were trying to contact. Don't be discouraged if you get nothing the first few times you try this. It may take a while for spirit to adjust to being "photographed" in this way. But do keep trying. You might see spots or flashes of light come out on the papers. You might see some strange imagery that needs to be studied and interpreted. But you should eventually see *something*, and something that you can relate to spirit.

One of the joys of the digital camera is that it doesn't use film. You can take innumerable photographs, and if you don't like any of them—or there is anything wrong with them—you can simply erase them and take more. This is an ideal setup for spirit photography.

There are two experiments you might try with a camera (digital or film). Set the camera on a tripod and focus on the area where you do your solitary séance. (If you are using a film camera, I recommend using a very fast film speed, at least 400 ASA.) If you have a remote release, or a timer release, then make use of it. Go through with one of your séances, be it table-tipping, psychometry, tarot, or whatever. At some point or points during the séance, trip the shutter of the camera. Do this a number of times. Afterward, review what you got. Many times it's just a picture of the setup, with nothing extraordinary. Sometimes—especially with digital cameras—there are a lot of orbs that appear. Occasionally—and this is what we are looking for—there is an "extra," a person in the photograph who was not physically present . . . spirit.

Yet another way of approaching this—again, especially with a digital camera so that you can take multiple exposures—is to set up the camera so that it is looking over your shoulder as you look into a mirror. With low light, and after your usual preparations, take a large number of photographs. You may be surprised to find—like Mary Todd Lincoln's discovery of Abraham's presence—a picture of spirit right there beside you in the picture.

ITC, EVP, and More

Instrumental transcommunication (ITC) includes various types of two-way interaction between the Spirit World and the Physical World using instruments such as the radio, telephone, tape recorder, computer, fax, and so on. It can include storable video as well as audio recording. While ITC is a two-way communication, electronic voice phenomena (EVP) refers to capturing spirit voices on tape or hearing them on the radio, telephone, or a tape. Although EVP is a useful tool for ghost hunting, ITC lends itself more to the subject matter of this book.

In 1982, a man named Klaus Schreiber started experimenting and set up a number of tape recorders in his basement. At one point he asked his deceased friend to speak to him, and almost immediately received a recording of his friend's voice greeting him. Schreiber went on to experiment with video cameras, simply focusing on one area of his basement and asking the spirits to show themselves. Fascinating videos taken from an inert television screen can be seen online, at YouTube, at the time of this writing. (Search "Klaus Schreiber.")

It isn't always easy to recognize a picture received in this way and it entails going painstakingly through tapes, frame by frame if necessary. One method is to connect a video camera to record a television screen that is tuned to a non-programmed channel—one that produces "snow" or pure blue screen. After about ten minutes of recording, go back and view the tape, examining it very slowly and carefully.

With both EVP and ITC, it is a slow and laborious process to get the spirit messages and/or images. Although it is possible to get responses to questions and comments, few people seem able to develop a regular two-way conversation, as such, with spirit. It is a far cry from the immediacy of such methods as talking boards, automatic writing, pendulums, and others we have covered. But instrumental transcommunication is a young science. The more people who become involved in it, the better the prospects for its development.

As mentioned in the sidebar in the chapter on runes, an old method of receiving messages was with two slates bound together. There is a modern version of this, using a computer, which I recommend trying. With either a desktop or laptop computer, open a new word-processing document file titled "Spirit Messages." If you have any question(s) or wish to connect with a specific spirit, then type in a greeting and give your question(s). Save it and then close the file. Also turn off the computer (it might be good to do this last

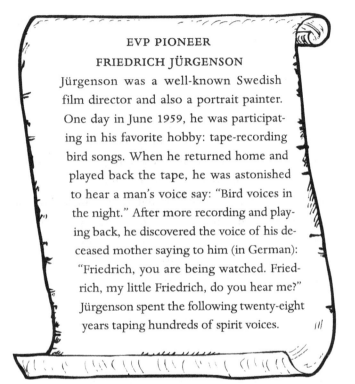

Jürgenson was a well-known Swedish film director and also a portrait painter. One day in June 1959, he was participating in his favorite hobby: tape-recording bird songs. When he returned home and played back the tape, he was astonished to hear a man's voice say: "Bird voices in the night." After more recording and playing back, he discovered the voice of his deceased mother saying to him (in German): "Friedrich, you are being watched. Friedrich, my little Friedrich, do you hear me?" Jürgenson spent the following twenty-eight years taping hundreds of spirit voices.

thing before shutting down the computer at the end of the day). Next time you start your computer, open the file and see if anything has been added. As with messages appearing on the slates, you may well find a message has appeared in your computer file.

Try this regularly. You may get nothing for a long time, but if you go through the process every night when you shut down, you may be surprised to find spirit accepting this method of contact and coming through to you.

When trying EVP with a tape recorder, if possible choose a recorder with two speeds. Record at the faster speed and play back at the slower speed. The spirit realm seems to operate on a higher frequency than does the physical world, and many times playing back at a slow speed allows you to hear things that are not picked up, or not obvious, when played back at the faster speed. It also helps to listen to the recording through headphones.

Digital recorders are the preferred type for EVP. The IC (integrated circuit) recorders are the best, and they do not need a microphone. If you are using a regular tape recorder, then make sure you have the best quality tape and a really good microphone. Use a plug-in microphone rather than just relying on a built-in one. Built-in microphones tend to pick up a slight hum from the machine.

❧

There are a tremendous number of methods used for divination that can be adapted for spirit communication, as has been shown. It is not necessary to detail each and every one of them, since most rely on interpreting symbols or perceived images. They can all, therefore, be related to the symbols we have addressed earlier in this book for such things as dreams, tasseography, and the like.

Try any method that you feel drawn to. For example, ceromancy (also known as ceroscopy) is the observation of hot wax dropped into water. When the wax hits the water, it gradually hardens into a variety of shapes. These shapes can be studied, and you can see what images they bring to mind. If you have prepared by doing your meditation, protection building, and concentration on a particular spirit, then you can relate these shapes to that spirit and make a connection.

The main thing to remember—and this is what separates this practice from simple divination—is to focus on contacting the departed spirit and to *know* that what you "see" is coming from that spirit. Daphnomancy was dependent upon the way in which a branch of laurel burned; geomancy is very much akin to tasseography; labiomancy, lampadomancy, ouranomancy, psephomancy, stercomancy, stolisomancy, and a host of others all follow similar lines. You can find a complete listing in my book *The Fortune-Telling Book: The Encyclopedia of Divination and Soothsaying*, if you are interested. However, in this book I have focused on what I feel to be the most tangible methods, especially with regard to immediacy of response from spirit.

Afterword

I have given a number of different methods for making contact with spirit when working alone. Not every method will work for everyone. Try them all and see which one, or ones, work best for you and concentrate there. However, there may be times when other methods you don't regularly employ do work and work well, so keep an open mind and don't limit yourself exclusively to your forte. Do keep records, as I've tried to stress throughout this book. And do take the trouble to check on what information comes through, so that you can acknowledge the validity of the spirit contact.

When the sum total of what you receive does not seem to match to anyone you can relate to yourself, then reach out to others near and dear to you—to friends, relations, co-workers. See if, perhaps, you are being used by spirit as an intermediary to carry an important word to someone who otherwise would have no idea how to make contact.

There are many ways to make contact with spirit. Variations on group activity can bring you new forms of solo connection. Don't hesitate to experiment, and to share your ideas with others.

Spiritualism Glossary

Not all of these terms are used in this book, but many of them are a part of Spiritualism as a whole and, as such, are included here.

Affirmations: Positive statements—usually brief—that are regularly repeated, thereby establishing them in the subconscious mind and reinforcing the conscious mind.

Astral plane: The spiritual dimension beyond the physical world. Nandor Fodor aligns it with the Second Level of Spiritualism, or "The first sphere after bodily death" (i.e., the Spirit World). It is the plane visited during sleep.

Automatic writing; drawing: Writing, drawing, or painting produced by spirit, when the conscious mind is otherwise engaged. Spirit makes use of the muscles of the arm and hand of the subject, who may be reading a book, watching television, talking with a friend, or doing any one of a number of tasks and is unaware of the spirit work.

Cabinet: A sectioned-off part of a séance room where the medium can consolidate the energy from the sitters. It may be a simple curtain across a corner of a room, or it may be a large wooden construction. With physical mediums, many times seemingly solid spirit figures will emerge and return to the cabinet. The medium may or may not be inside the cabinet.

Channeling: Acting as an intermediary to bring information directly from an entity in another dimension. In effect, mediumship is a form of channeling, but the term is more generally applied to those who channel information from nonphysical beings, who may or may not have previously lived on this plane, rather than from the deceased spirits of family members.

Circle: The term given to a sitting, or séance, or to a development group, since the usual form is to sit in a circle of chairs. These chairs may or may not be around a table.

Clairalience: Literally, "clear smelling." Many times a perfume, or the smell of a cigar, or another scent is recognized in a circle. To smell something of the Spirit World is, then, known as clairalience.

Clairaudience: Meaning "clear hearing," this is the ability to hear sounds, music, and voices from the world of spirit.

These are not audible to normal ears but are picked up by mediums.

Clairgustance; clairhambience: To get a taste in the mouth, coming from spirit.

Clairsentience: Meaning "clear sensing." Without actually "seeing" or "hearing," a medium can sense information being brought by spirit. It is a psychic perception of information—be it sounds, smells, names, dates, dress, etc.

Clairvoyance: Meaning "clear seeing," it is the ability of a medium to see, in his or her mind's eye, spirits, and to see scenes and other information being brought to sitters at a séance.

Control: A term sometimes applied to a spirit guide, or gatekeeper, though "control" is something of a misnomer since it does not actually control the medium. However, it may control the order in which spirits come through to the medium.

Development circle: A group of like-minded people who wish to develop their mediumistic abilities. They usually meet on a regular schedule and work on various psychic development exercises. Also known as a *home circle*.

Doorkeeper: The main spirit of a medium, who acts as a screen for the medium at a séance, regulating which spirits are allowed to come through. Also known as a *gatekeeper*, *life guide*, *control*, and similar terms.

Guide: A spirit who watches over a living person. Each person may have any number of such guides, with some being specific to a specific task such as healing. The guide may act as gatekeeper at a séance, arranging who should come through and when.

Infinite Intelligence: Sometimes referred to as "Mother/Father God," this is a Spiritualist term for the incomprehensible power of the universe.

Inspirational writing: Writing from inspirational thoughts received from spirit rather than from conscious composition. In automatic writing, the writing is actually done by spirit, utilizing a person's arm and hand; in inspirational writing, the writing is consciously done by the person, but the thoughts and words come from spirit. It might be equated to taking spirit dictation!

Levitation: To raise up an object contrary to the known laws of gravity. It is a phenomenon of *psychokinesis* (PK), or causing objects to move without physical contact with them. Examples of levitation are usually seen in the presence of physical mediums. Occasionally, table-tipping can lead to the levitating of the table.

Manifestation (or Materialization): The appearance of a spirit, in visible form, usually at a séance. It may be in solid form or it may be transparent, as an apparition. A spontaneous manifestation can occur under various conditions and be regarded as a "ghost."

ALLAN KARDEC

Allan Kardec (1804–69) was born in Lyon, France. His real name was Hippolyte Léon Denizard Rivail. He was fascinated by table-tipping when it came to France in 1850, and held a number of séances with two sisters who were mediums. Rivail was not himself a medium but was told, through the sisters, that he should publish his research on life after death, using the nom de plume Allan Kardec—two names he'd had in previous lives, according to the spirits. He published several books. Most notable are *The Spirits' Book* (1857) and *The Mediums' Book* (1861). He promoted the idea of reincarnation but was reluctant to acknowledge physical mediumship, despite the evidence of many prominent physical mediums. His version of/ideas about Spiritualism caught on throughout France and became known as *Spiritism*. His books and teachings also flourished in South America, especially Brazil, and in the Philippines, where there is a great deal of Spiritist activity today.

Medium: A person sensitive to the vibrations of the Spirit World. By adjusting his or her vibrations—consciously or unconsciously—a bridge is established between the two worlds, enabling spirit to communicate with those of this world. Mediumship is an ancient and universal practice, found throughout history in all parts of the world.

Mental phenomena: This includes clairvoyance, clairaudience, clairsentience, psychometry, scrying, and various forms of healing. Mental mediumship is subjective.

Natural law: The principles of nature, which includes humankind along with all forms of life: animal, vegetable, and mineral. Understanding of the natural law determines our actions and reactions. It's possible to create our own realities by the choices we make.

Physical phenomena: These include levitation, direct voice communication, apports, automatic writing, talking boards and planchettes, table-tipping, trumpets, slate writing, manifestations, transfiguration, rappings, and knockings. Physical mediumship is objective.

Planchette: A small platform used with a talking board—such as a Ouija® board—or, with a pencil in it, used for automatic writing.

Platform: A stage from which mediums may deliver messages.

Possession: Possession takes place when a spirit or entity takes over the body of another, without that person's permission. (It is not as common as some movies would have us believe!)

Precognition: To know ahead of time.

Psychic: To know information by sensing it; a person who obtains knowledge without having normal access to it, through extrasensory perception. All mediums are psychic though not all psychics are mediums.

Psychometry: From the Greek *psyche* ("soul") and *metron* ("measure"). This is the handling of an object and, from its vibrations, picking up information about its history: owner(s), origin, value, etc.

Rapping: Knocking noises produced by spirit. The origins of Spiritualism date from the rappings made by the spirit of the murdered peddler Charles B. Rosna, communicating with the Fox sisters in 1848.

Reading: The giving of information by a medium, or a psychic, to a sitter. It implies that the mind/vibrations of the sitter are being "read." A psychic may actually read a palm, tarot cards, runes, or other objects to focus his or her mind. A medium would "read" from the information provided by spirits.

Retrocognition: Knowledge of things from the past, by other than normal means.

Skrying (also **Scrying**): Using a reflective surface as a focal point for seeing the past, present, or future. Crystal balls are common objects for skrying, but polished metals, ink blots, water, and any other reflective surfaces have been, and are, used by skryers around the world.

Séance: Literally a "sitting." It is a sitting with a medium for the purpose of communicating with the spirits of the dead. Depending upon the type of medium (mental or physical) and the sorts of phenomena expected, the séance is conducted in bright light, subdued light, or even in complete darkness.

Skotograph: A name given to some spirit-produced photographs, usually produced on raw photographic paper without the aid of a camera.

Slate: The same as the old schoolroom slates used for writing but in Spiritualism used in pairs, fastened together face to face, with a piece of chalk between them. Left out at a séance, spirit may produce writing on one or both of the slates.

Spirit: Generally used in the sense of the essence of a person that moves on from the physical body to the ethereal. It is the post-deceased aspect that communicates, from the Spirit World, with earthly people.

Spiritism, Spiritist: Terms introduced and used by Allan Kardec in place of the words *Spiritualism* and *Spiritualist*, for his representation of the beliefs and philosophies of the religion. These terms were used in Kardec's native France (in French: *spiritisme, spirite*), and their equivalents are still used extensively in South America (especially Brazil) and the Philippines.

Spirit photography: The capturing of spirit forms in photographs, either accidentally or on purpose.

Spiritualism: The religion, science, and philosophy that teach a belief in a continuous life, based upon communication with those who have progressed to the Spirit World. Contact is made through the agencies of a medium. The main tenet of Spiritualism is what is termed the "Golden Rule."

Spiritualist: One who practices Spiritualism. A Spiritualist may or may not be a medium.

Summerland: Term coined by Andrew Jackson Davis (see the first sidebar in the "Preliminaries" chapter) for the afterlife; the world of spirit.

Synchronicity: Events that happen simultaneously, or near-simultaneously, that appear to be coincidental and meaningful.

Talking board: A board, usually marked off with the letters of the alphabet, numbers, and short phrases, that is used for communicating with spirit. The sliding pointer of the board is known as a planchette and its movement is directed by spirit. The best-known commercially produced board is the Ouija® board.

Trance: An altered state of consciousness in which the brainwave activity moves to a certain level. There are basically four such levels: *beta, alpha, theta,* and *delta.* Beta is the normal, wide-awake level. The next level down is the alpha level (what might be termed a "light" trance). Below that is theta, and the deepest level (the equivalent of somnambulism in hypnosis) is delta, a deep trance state. Mediums enter into various levels of trance, consciously or unconsciously.

Bibliography

Barbanell, Maurice. *This Is Spiritualism*. Oxshott, UK: The Spiritual Truth Press, 1959.

Berkowitz, Rita S., and Deborah S. Romaine. *The Complete Idiot's Guide to Communicating with Spirits*. Indianapolis, IN: Alpha Books, 2003.

Besterman, Theodore. *Crystal-Gazing*. London: Rider, 1924.

Bodian, Stephan. *Meditation for Dummies, 2nd edition*. Hoboken, NJ: Wiley, 2006.

Bro, Harmon H. *Edgar Cayce on Dreams*. New York: Warner Books, 1968.

Buckland, Raymond. *The Buckland Gypsies' Domino Divination Deck*. St. Paul, MN: Llewellyn, 1999.

————. *Buckland's Book of Spirit Communications*. St. Paul, MN: Llewellyn, 2004.

————. *Buckland's Complete Gypsy Fortuneteller*. St. Paul, MN: Llewellyn, 1997.

————. *Buckland's Domino Divination*. Los Angeles: Pendraig Publishing, 2010.

————. *The Fortune-Telling Book: The Encyclopedia of Divination and Soothsaying*. Detroit, MI: Visible Ink Press, 2004.

————. *Gypsy Dream Dictionary*, 2nd edition. St. Paul, MN: Llewellyn, 1999.

————. *Ouija—"Yes! Yes!"* Fortuna, CA: Doorway Publications, 2006.

————. *The Spirit Book: The Encyclopedia of Clairvoyance, Channeling, and Spirit Communication*. Detroit, MI: Visible Ink Press 2006.

Cull, Robert. *More to Life Than This: The Story of Jean Cull*. London: Macmillan, 1987.

Doyle, Arthur Conan. *The History of Spiritualism*. New York: Doran, 1926.

Edward, John. *Crossing Over: The Stories Behind the Stories*. New York: Princess Books, 2001.

Edwards, Harry. *A Guide for the Development of Mediumship*. Greenford, UK: Con-Psy Publications, 2003.

Elliott, Ralph W. V. *Runes: An Introduction*. Westport, CT: Greenwood Press, 1981. (Originally published in the UK by Manchester University Press in 1959.)

Flint, Leslie. *Voices in the Dark: My Life as a Medium*. New York: Bobbs-Merrill, 1971.

Fodor, Nandor. *Encyclopedia of Psychic Science*. London: Arthur's Press, 1933.

Gray, Eden. *The Tarot Revealed*. New York: Inspiration House, 1960.

Grimshaw, Thomas. *General Course of the History, Science, Philosophy and Religion of Spiritualism*. Milwaukee, WI: Morris Pratt Institute, 1973.

Guiley, Rosemary Ellen. *The Encyclopedia of Ghosts and Spirits*. New York: Facts on File, 1992

Martin, Joel, and Patricia Romanowski. *We Don't Die*. New York: Putnam, 1988.

Matthews, Mary W. "The Difference Between Soul and Spirit" (2010). ExtremelySmart.com. Online at www.extremely smart.com/insight/theology/soul&spirit.php. © 2010.

Mermet, Abbé. *Principles and Practice of Radiesthesia*. London: Watkins, 1975.

Moses, William Stainton. *Direct Spirit Writing*. London: L. N. Fowler, 1878.

Mühl, Anita M. *Automatic Writing*. New York: Helix Press, 1963. (Originally published in Germany in 1930.)

Mumler, William H. *The Personal Experiences of William H. Mumler in Spirit-Photography*. Boston: Colby and Rich, 1875.

Nagy, Ron. *Slate Writing: Invisible Intelligence*. Lakeville, MN: Galde Press, 2008.

National Spiritualist Association of Churches. *NSAC Spiritualist Manual*. Lily Dale, NY: NSAC, 2002.

Northage, Ivy. *Mechanics of Mediumship*. London: College of Psychic Studies, 1973.

———. *Mediumship Made Simple*. London: College of Psychic Studies, 1986.

Obley, Carole J. *I'm Still with You: True Stories of Healing Grief Through Spirit Communication*. Ropley, UK: O Books, 2008.

Owens, Elizabeth. *How to Communicate with Spirits*. St. Paul, MN: Llewellyn, 2001.

Putnam, Betty L. *History of Lily Dale*. Lily Dale, NY: Lily Dale Historical Society, [no date].

Sherman, Harold. *You Can Communicate with the Unseen World*. New York: Fawcett, 1974.

Steiger, Brad. *Voices from Beyond: True Incidents Indicative of Life Beyond Death*. New York: Award Books, 1968.

Walsch, Neale Donald. *Conversations with God*. New York: G. P. Putnam's Sons, 1996.

Yost, Casper S. *Patience Worth: A Psychic Mystery*. New York: Henry Holt, 1916.

Zolar. *Zolar's Book of the Spirits: All the Most Famous and Fabulous Lore about Contacting the Spirit World*. New York: Prentice Hall, 1987.

Illustration credits

Border on pages v, ix, 1, 11, 27, 41, 71, 77, 85, 87, 97, 101, 109, 117, 129, 153, 159, 165, 187, 193, 197, 205, 213, 215, and 225 from *Art Explosion Image Library* (2004).

Scroll on pages 2, 5, 14, 16–17, 21, 32, 36, 38, 93, 105, 114, 127, 132, 200, 209, and 219 from *Art Explosion Image Library* (2004).

Illustration on page 41 from *A Treasury of Bookplates*. Fridolf Johnson, editor. (Dover Publications, 1977.)

Photograph on page 71 from *Mysterious Psychic Forces* by Camille Flammarion (London: T. Fisher Unwin, 1907).

Illustrations on pages 77, 85, 89, 117 and 129 from *Hands: A Pictorial Archive from Nineteenth-Century Sources*. Jim Harter, editor. (Dover Publications, 1985.)

Illustrations on pages 89, 101, and 141 from *Montgomery Ward & Co. 1895 Catalogue Facsimile* (Dover Publications, 1969).

Illustration on page 97 from *Science and Literature in the Middle Ages* (Paul Lacroix, 1878).

Illustrations on pages 107, 120 and 135 by the Llewellyn Art Department.

Illustration on page 109 from *The Magus* by Francis Barrett (1801).

Illustrations on pages 153, 159, 187, 191, 197, and 205 from *Harter's Picture Archive* (Dover Publications, 1978).

Illustration on page 165 from *Food and Drink: A Pictorial Archive from Nineteenth-Century Sources*. (Dover Publications, 1979).

Illustration on page 190 from *Advanced Candle Magick* © 1996 Raymond Buckland. (St. Paul, MN: Llewellyn Publications, 2002.)

Illustration on page 193 from *Symbols Signs & Signets* (Dover Publications, 1950).

To Write to the Author

If you wish to contact the author or would like more information about this book, please write to the author in care of Llewellyn Worldwide and we will forward your request. Both the author and publisher appreciate hearing from you and learning of your enjoyment of this book and how it has helped you. Llewellyn Worldwide cannot guarantee that every letter written to the author can be answered, but all will be forwarded. Please write to:

Raymond Buckland
℅ Llewellyn Worldwide
2143 Wooddale Drive
Woodbury, MN 55125-2989

Please enclose a self-addressed stamped envelope for reply,
or $1.00 to cover costs. If outside the USA, enclose
an international postal reply coupon.

Many of Llewellyn's authors have websites with additional information and resources. For more information, please visit our website at http://www.llewellyn.com.